D0530145

AS Level Health & Social Care

REVISION GUIDE

Unit 1: Human Growth and Development

Karen Lancaster

MERTHYR TYDFIL COLLEGE
LIBRARY

MERTHYR TYDFIL COLLEGE

26215

Lulu Publishing
Lulu Enterprises, Inc.
860 Aviation Parkway, Suite 300
Morrisville, NC 27560, USA
http://www.lulu.com/

© 2007 Karen Lancaster

ISBN 978-1-84753-369-2

10   9   8   7   6   5   4   3   2   1

All rights reserved. No part of this publication may be reproduced, stored in a retrieval system, or transmitted in any form or by any means, electronic, mechanical, photocopying, recording or otherwise, without the prior written permission of the Publisher, or as expressly permitted by law, or a licence permitting restricted copying in the United Kingdom issued by the Copyright Licensing Agency Ltd., 90 Tottenham Court Road, London, W1T 4LP.

You must not circulate this book in any other binding or cover and you must impose this same condition on any acquirer.

Published by Lulu.
The publisher accepts no responsibility for any material published on websites referred to in this book.

Website addresses in this book were correct at the time of going to press, but be aware that these can change at any time.

Acknowledgements
The author would like to thank everybody involved in the production of this book. This includes teachers, students and assessors who gave feedback on the early drafts. Photographs courtesy of Callisto Photographic Database. Cartoons provided by Humbug. Technical assistance from Ken Anderson. Cover design by Bomber. Special thanks also to Sandra Sidebottom for her patient and diligent copyediting skills.

The case studies and names used in this book are entirely fictitious. Any resemblance to any persons, living or dead, is entirely coincidental.

Ganymede House

CONTENTS

ABOUT THIS BOOK

This book is written especially for students who are taking the AS Single Award or AS Double Award in Health and Social Care with Edexcel. It is a revision guide which recaps all the vital information you will need to perform well in the external examination for *Unit 1: Human Growth and Development*. All students need to sit this examination.

This book is no substitute for attending lessons, listening to your teachers, and working hard! It is not the intention of this book to teach you things from scratch: what this book can do, however, is help you focus your revision and develop your exam technique in order for you to get the grade you are capable of.

The book has been split into five main sections to help you focus your studies:
- **Revision & Examinations**
- **Fast Facts**
- **Sample Examination Papers**
- **Mark Schemes**
- **Completed Exams**

The **Revision & Examinations** section gives you general information about how to go about revising, and how to prepare for examinations. There is also specific information about the *Unit 1: Human Growth and Development* examination, including how to manage your time and structure your answers.

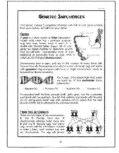

The **Fast Facts** section will recap all the basic information you need to have a good grounding in the subject. You should try to ensure that you can remember as much of this information as possible before you attempt the Sample Examination Papers.

Use the **Sample Examination Papers** to test yourself under timed exam conditions: choose one paper, and avoid the temptation to pick and mix questions from each of the papers. Give yourself 1½ hours and answer as many of the questions as you can, as fully and accurately as you would do in the real examination. The Sample Examination Papers are written in the same style as the real exam questions are, so this is excellent practice for you.

The **Mark Schemes** section provides a guide for marking the Sample Examination Papers. When you have completed one of the papers, mark your answers using the relevant Mark Scheme. Don't be too lenient with yourself – the external assessors won't be. But nor will they try to catch you out, or be completely inflexible. Use a degree of judgement about just how similar your answer is to that given in the Mark Scheme. You may need to refer to the Fast Facts section to check the accuracy of some of your answers, or ask a teacher.

Once you have completed one full Sample Examination Paper, consider how well you did. If you did badly, it could be a good idea to have another go at the same Sample Examination Paper at a later date.

Work out what (if anything) was your downfall:
- Were you inaccurate on the short, factual answers?
- Did you go off on a tangent in the longer discussion questions?
- Were your discussions too one-sided?
- Did you struggle to find enough things to say (e.g. for each area of development)?
- Did you fail to give enough information when asked to explain something?
- Did you struggle to interpret the sources?

Of course, perhaps you did exceedingly well, in which case, you should be very pleased with yourself. Test yourself with the other Sample Examination Papers at a later date and see if you do as well on all of them. If you are doing exceptionally well, it may be worth considering whether you are marking yourself fairly, or whether you are being too kind towards yourself. (On the other hand, maybe you are just a genius?!)

The more you know about your own strengths and weaknesses, the better you will be able to brush up on your weak areas, and perform really well in the real examination.

The Mark Schemes simply give you a guide about how to mark the papers, and they do not show how you should structure your answers in order to get a grade A. There are lots of different things a person could write in order to get a grade A, but to give you an idea, you should look at the Completed Exams section.

The **Completed Exams** section shows you precisely that. Two sets of answers to one of the Sample Examination Papers are compared side by side: one set of answers would achieve approximately a grade E, whilst the other would get a grade A. You should look at the differences in the way questions were approached, and the detail and explanations given. Be sure to read the examiner's comments in the margins, to see why certain answers did well (or badly). Once you can tell the difference between  a good answer and a bad answer, you are one step closer to producing the good answers yourself, and getting that grade A.

At the end, there is a **Further Reading** section: if you feel that you want to broaden your knowledge further, any of the books or websites included in this section could be useful to you.

Revision & Examinations

This section gives you some general guidance about revision and examinations: this will probably help you in *all* your subjects. You will find out hints and tips for planning your revision, and focusing your time in the examinations. You will also learn how to structure your answers and write effectively.

REVISION

Revision is often boring, but it has to be done! Don't make the mistake of thinking you can excel without putting the hours in: it just won't happen. Here are some general Dos and Don'ts that apply no matter what subjects you are studying:

Do

✓ **Make flash cards** and use them to test yourself: E.g. write "Growth" on one side of the card, and on the other, write "a physical increase in height or weight". Do this for lots of things. To test yourself, look at the side which says "Growth", and try to define what it is. Then turn over the card to see if you were right. Put the ones you get right into one pile, and the ones you get wrong into another. When you have gone through all the cards, go back to the 'wrong' pile, and try them again. Keep doing this until you have got all of them right.

✓ **Draw spider diagrams** to see it all mapped out. This is really useful if you are a visual learner. Use highlighter pens, little drawings, shapes, diagrams, symbols or arrows – anything that will help the information stick in your mind. Then when you remember a certain word, you could be able to mentally 'see' what is written next to it.

✓ **Revise in other ways**: if flash cards and spider diagrams don't work for you, use any other methods you can to get things stuck in your head. Use mnemonics (e.g. "Never Eat Shredded Wheat", to remember that the compass points are north, east, south and west). Sometimes simply repeating things over and over, or writing them out ten (or more) times is enough to make you remember it. Persevere and see what works for you.

✓ **Practice writing**. For many of your exams you'll need to be writing for one or two hours non-stop. It's no good knowing it all in your mind if your hand is in too much pain to write it down. If you were going to run a marathon, you would need to train by running: your hand muscles are going to do a lot of exercise in your exams, so you need to make sure they are fully 'fit'. If you find your hand aches after taking notes for half an hour in a lesson, you need to get your writing hand in training!

✓ **Give yourself regular breaks** and rewards – e.g. "when I've revised for an hour, I can watch TV for twenty minutes" or "if I get more than 60% on this practice test, I will buy myself a bar of chocolate". But don't cheat or break your promises to yourself!!

✓ **Set yourself intermediate deadlines.** E.g. to have completed one past paper by a certain date. This way you'll know whether you are on track to complete all your revision in time for the exam (and if you're running behind schedule, you'll know to speed up and work harder.)

<u>DON'T</u>

✗ **Don't just read things** – it won't sink in. This is the mantra of teachers all over the country, and still many students think they have 'learnt' something simply because they have read it. If only this were true, we would all be absolute geniuses. Reading is very easy, but the only way to know whether you have learnt it is by testing yourself, by covering it over and repeating it, using flash cards, and by sitting practice papers.

✗ **Don't let your breaks last too long.** This is a fairly obvious one. A reward such as "when I've revised for an hour, I can watch twenty minutes of TV" is a good incentive, but don't start saying "when I've revised for ten minutes, I can go shopping for four hours".

✗ **Don't spend ages drawing up a revision timetable** – you'll almost certainly ignore it! Revision timetables are just procrastination in disguise. Just make a basic checklist so you can tick off the topics as you cover them. Rather than spend time planning how you'll revise, just revise!

✗ **Don't leave it till the last minute.** You need to start revising three or four weeks before the examination: earlier, if you have more than one exam. Last-minute cramming is only useful *on top of* weeks of preparation. Last-minute cramming alone is relatively useless.

✗ **Don't get distracted** by things around you such as TV, family, loud music, the weather, etc. If you get easily distracted, go somewhere quiet which you find really boring – e.g. a public library. There, the most interesting thing for you to do will be revision, so this'll make you much less likely to get distracted.

× **Don't "revise" with friends** if you don't get much actual work done. It's very easy to think you are revising because you all have an open textbook in front of you, but it's only revision if you can remember more at the end of the session than you could at the start. One thing you *can* do with friends is to test each other using flash cards, or mark each other's Sample Examination Papers.

Revision is your key to success. No normal person can remember everything they did in lessons without recapping it. If you don't revise properly, you might forget whole sections. If, during your revision, you realise there is something you missed, for example if you were off sick, then it is well worth borrowing notes from a friend, or asking your teacher what work you missed so that you can catch up.

EXAMINATIONS

The examinations are the culmination of all your hard work: don't throw it all away by making silly mistakes.

Do

✓ **Turn up on time to exams**. This really means turning up ten minutes early, so that you are seated, calm and collected when the examination starts. Don't be searching round in your bag or panicking about where you are supposed to sit: turn up early and get yourself sorted out in time for the start of the exam.

✓ **Bring yourself a drink** and a light snack if you have several back-to-back exams. If you are allowed to eat food during the examination, take something simple and quiet to eat: choose a cereal bar or chocolate bar as opposed to a bag of crisps. Drink little and often, but don't drink so much that you'll need the toilet during the exam.

✓ **Bring two or three pens**, in case one or more runs out. Remember that you need to write all exams in blue or black ink. Do not write in any other colour. This is really important. Many exam boards have special rules in place that say only the examiner can write in red or green: if you write in pencil, or red or green (or any other colour) ink then your examination script may have to be marked by a different person. This really annoys examiners, and they frown upon anyone silly enough to write their exam in the wrong colour pen. Write in blue or black ink; nothing else, (unless you are drawing a graph or diagram.)

✓ **Manage your time**. The exam takes 1½ hours (90 minutes) and there are 90 marks available. This equates to one mark per minute. So for a question worth 5 marks, you should spend 5 minutes on it. You will probably need to spend longer than ten minutes on 10 mark questions, and less than two minutes on 2 mark questions, but the mark-per-minute is a useful guide. Don't spend 25 minutes on a question worth 10 marks.

✓ **Turn off your mobile phone**. You can be instantly failed if your mobile goes off during an examination – whether or not you answer it. Turn your mobile phone off, and leave it in your bag at the front of the hall.

✓ **Read the question properly**, and at the end of each point you make, check you are actually *answering* it! It is amazing how many candidates throw away easy marks by half-reading a question, and then launching straight into answering it – or rather, answering what they *think* the question is.

DON'T

× **Don't drink any alcohol** (or take drugs!) the night before an exam. Alcohol and illegal drugs can *never* improve your performance in an exam. Sitting your A-Level exams with a hangover would be a ridiculously stupid thing to do, as there is no way you can give it your full concentration. (Plus, as you are a Health and Social Care student, you will know all about the bad things that alcohol and drugs can do to your body, so you shouldn't be taking either of them anyway!)

× **Don't leave the exam early**. There is absolutely nothing to be gained by leaving early: you are given 1½ hours to do the exam because that is the amount of time the examiners think it would take a good candidate to get a grade A. If you are anything less than perfect, you will need to make use of all the time available to get the best possible marks. If you think you have finished, go back and re-read all your answers; see if there is anything else you can add. Even if you spend half an hour sitting and thinking, and you only manage to come up with another couple of points, it could still make the difference between an A and a B (or an E and a Fail!)

× **Don't take too long on breaks**. If you have back-to-back exams, with a short break in between them, don't take too long on the break. There's probably *not* enough time for a whole cigarette, or to queue up and buy a sandwich. Use your break times to go to the toilet and gather your thoughts ready for the next exam. The examiner may start without you if you're late back.

Good luck with your exams. If there is anything you are unsure about, ask your teacher before the exam. It's better to look a bit of an idiot by asking a silly question beforehand, than it is to look a *complete* idiot by failing the exam because you didn't know something vital.

HUMAN GROWTH AND DEVELOPMENT: THE EXAMINATION

Doing well in the exam is important: it counts for 33% of your final A-Level grade. To achieve well in the examination, it is important that you learn the *entire* content of the syllabus in order for you to apply this knowledge in the questions. However, the exam is not simply about regurgitating information; it is about being able to give full, accurate and well-argued answers to a range of short and long questions.

The examination paper is split into three sections; each will be worth approximately 30 marks:

Section 1 This section includes:
- ★ Growth
- ★ Life stages
- ★ Self-concept
- ★ Relationships
- ★ Physical, intellectual, language, social and emotional development
- ★ Gross and fine motor skills
- ★ Puberty

Section 2 This section includes:
- ★ Lifestyles
- ★ Nature/ nurture
- ★ Environmental factors
- ★ Genetic factors
- ★ Smoking, drinking, drugs, diet and exercise
- ★ Race, class and ethnicity
- ★ Social factors

Section 3 This section includes:
- ★ Definitions of health
- ★ Barriers to health
- ★ Public health
- ★ Health studies, surveys and trends
- ★ Health promotion campaigns
- ★ Health effects on development

(The sections will not necessarily be in this order, and there may be some crossover between sections.)

Each section carries roughly equal weighting, so you need to ensure that you have studied each section in equal detail. This includes section 3, which candidates sometimes fail to study in depth.

THE EXAMINATION

The exam will **not** look like the Sample Examination Papers given on pages 74 to 84 of this book. To see what the examination will actually look like, look at the Completed Exams section on pages 108 to 131 (the examination paper will be A4 size).

In the exam, you should answer your questions in the spaces provided. If there is not enough room for you to complete your answer in the booklet, you should ask for extra paper on which to continue your answers, and make sure you number all your questions clearly. As a rough guide, you should be writing approximately one page of A4 for a 10-mark question, and half a page of A4 for a 5-mark question, depending on the size of your handwriting.

The exam lasts for 1½ hours, and you should write as much as you can during this time. For most long questions (but not all of them – see below), you will not be penalised for giving more information than required, so it makes sense to write as much as possible on these.

You should expect to get several short questions (worth 1 to 5 marks) as well as several longer questions (worth 8 to 12 marks). The total number of marks available for the paper is 90.

WHAT TO WRITE

Questions which begin "**Explain**..." require you to give more information about something, to clarify the issue. Don't give advantages or disadvantages: just an explanation.

"**Evaluate**..." "**Assess**..." or "**Discuss**..." questions are where you ought to write about the advantages and disadvantages of an issue; for these questions, you should make as many points as there are marks available. This means that if the question is worth 8 marks, you should make 8 points. It is acceptable to bullet point, but make sure that you use full sentences and give a complete answer, linking your sentences together. You should also ensure that you present a balanced argument, consisting of some positive points and some negative points: do not focus on just the good or just the bad. Even something such as drug abuse can bring benefits, and something such as getting married can bring drawbacks.

For (e.g.) a 6-mark question which states: "**Explain three reasons**..." you should of course only state three reasons, but explain yourself fully by giving further information on the points you raise. Do *not* make more than three points though, or your could actually lose marks

For a question such as "**Discuss the effects of ... on development**" which is worth eight or more marks, you should aim to make at least one negative and one positive point for each area of development (physical, intellectual, emotional and social.)

Before you start to answer the first question in a section, it is worth looking at *all* the questions for that section. Many candidates duplicate parts of their answers, simply because they have not read question (b) before they start answering question (a). You will never be required to duplicate answers, so if you find you are doing, you must be missing something important. Re-read both questions and work out what each is asking you for.

As well as the Sample Examination Papers given in this book, you should ask your Health and Social Care teacher to give you a copy of the past papers; (these are not available online.) Practicing past papers and the Sample Examination Papers in this book will be the best preparation you can get for doing well in the real examination.

For further information, visit the Edexcel website at: www.edexcel.org.uk/quals/gce /hsc/adv/ 9741/ and look at the following documents:
- *the Specification*
- *the Specimen Paper with Mark Scheme,*
- *the Teacher's Guide*
- *all the Examiners Reports*

Fast Facts

This section contains a wealth of facts and information that you will need to understand for the examination. Tables and bullet points are used to make it simple and fast for you to find the information you need.

All words which are highlighted in **bold** in the Fast Facts section can be found in the Glossary on pages 134-140.

> **Be careful!**
> *Look out for the "Be careful!" boxes. They warn you of some common errors made by candidates: don't fall victim to these mistakes!*

GROWTH AND DEVELOPMENT

- ♦ **Growth** is the physical changes in height, size and weight that occur in a person

- ♦ **Development** is an increase in skills or abilities: this includes all the other changes that occur in a person. There are four types of development, which can be remembered using the word **PIES**:

Physical	Intellectual	Emotional	Social
e.g. motor skills, co-ordination, balance	e.g. language, maths, colours	e.g. controlling one's own feelings	e.g. bonding with family / friends

Be careful!
Simply getting taller is **not** physical development: getting taller is growth. Physical development is improving your physical skills.

HOW IS GROWTH MEASURED?

Growth can be measured using a **centile chart**, to see how someone's height or weight compares to the **norm** (the expected growth pattern) for someone their age. A centile chart will often show the 5th, 50th, and 95th centiles. The 50th centile line shows the average height or weight of people of any given age. Ninety-five percent of people will fall below the 95th centile line, and only 5% of people will fall below the 5th centile line. For example, the graph shows a three year old boy who is 100cm tall: he falls above the 50th centile, so he is taller than at least 50% of other three year old boys.

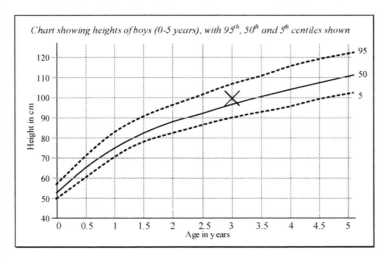

Chart showing heights of boys (0-5 years), with 95th, 50th and 5th centiles shown

HOW IS DEVELOPMENT MEASURED?

Development is harder to measure than growth. Physical development is measured by seeing whether someone can do a particular task; e.g. walking, kicking a ball, holding a pencil. Intellectual development is measured through tests and projects throughout schooling and often into employment. Emotional and social development are harder to measure, but differences can often be seen in people's reactions to new or tense situations, large groups of people and relationships with others. Adults are much better at controlling or hiding their emotions than children are.

Growth and development are necessary because children are too small, weak and immature to carry out adult tasks: a period of growth and development up until the age of 18 or older will see individuals becoming physically, mentally, socially and emotionally capable of carrying out jobs in society.

LIFE STAGES

0 – 2 **Infancy**
2 – 8 **Childhood**
9 – 18 **Adolescence**

19+ **Adulthood**
- **Early Adulthood** 19 – 45
- **Middle Adulthood** 45 – 65
- **Later Adulthood** 65+

> **Be careful!**
> Later Adulthood is also known as Old Age, but the term "Later Adulthood" is preferred because it's more PC and not as offensive.

PHYSICAL GROWTH AND DEVELOPMENT

Physical growth and development refers to the visible and non-visible physical changes that occur in a person throughout their **life span** (the length of time they are alive for). People usually grow in height and weight until the age of 17 or 18; after this age, height remains the same, but weight and abilities may alter depending on the individual's **lifestyle**.

At birth, the average baby is 50cm long and weighs 7lb 3oz. A newborn baby is the largest it can be, whilst still being able to fit through the birth canal. A newborn baby's head is quite large in comparison to its body; after birth, the head grows at a slower rate than the rest of the body, so that by the time someone is an adult, their head is much smaller in comparison to the size of their body.

Maturation

Maturation is a process of physical growth and development: it is like a "body clock" which tells your body when to go through certain stages. Bee and Bjorklund (2007) found 3 characteristics of maturation: it is universal, sequential and biological:

Universal	It happens to all people in all cultures	*e.g. menstruation happens to women all over the world, regardless of where or how they live*
Sequential	It happens in an expected and understandable pattern	*e.g. a child will learn to crawl before he learns to walk*
Biological	It does not rely on anything in the environment to make it happen	*e.g. a man will get hairy armpits whether or not he has been educated in school*

INTELLECTUAL DEVELOPMENT

Intellectual or **cognitive** development refers to the way a person learns and thinks, and the improvements in their knowledge or mental capabilities. Family, schooling and employment are the main sources of intellectual development in a person's life; early education is particularly important. Intellectual development can continue into old age and up until death.

Swiss psychologist Jean Piaget recognised four stages of intellectual development in children:

Stage	Age	Key issue
Sensory motor	0 – 2 years	Babies learn about the world through their senses. They are **egocentric** – they see the world from their viewpoint only. At around 8 months they develop **object permanence**: they know that things still exist even if they are out of sight.

Pre-operational (pre-logic)	2 – 7 years	Children do not think in a logical way; they are still egocentric. They express themselves through language. They think that objects and animals have the same emotions as humans.
Concrete operational	7 – 11 years	Children can see things from others' points of view; this is called **decentring**. They can understand logic if they can see or handle objects. They do not fully understand logical arguments which are only explained in words. They understand that objects do not have feelings, and animals have limited emotions.
Formal operational	11+ years	People can understand logical arguments and can think in an abstract way. They can solve logic problems in their head without objects. (Most people will reach this stage, but people with learning disabilities may not.)

LANGUAGE DEVELOPMENT

Learning to speak and understand language is part of intellectual development. Children learn whatever language(s) they hear – many children learn two or more languages simultaneously from birth; they are **bilingual** or **multilingual**.

There are several stages a child will pass through to learn language:-

Stage	Features	Examples
Pre-linguistic stage (6 - 12 months)	The baby starts babbling and making language-like sounds, but there are no words and no meanings attached to the sounds	"ma... ma... ma..." "babababababab" "dededededede"
Linguistic stage (12 - 18 months)	The baby can say a few 'words', which have meanings attached to them	"mama" can mean *mummy*
Holophrases (12 - 18 months)	The baby will use one word to mean several (relevant) things	"teddy" means *look at the teddy'* or *'where's my teddy?'*
Telegraphic speech (18 - 24 months)	The infant forms two-word 'sentences' that have meaning and are understood	"Nana gone"; "Where car?"; "Want tea"
Virtuous errors (2 - 4 years)	The child says meaningful sentences, but there are still some grammatical errors	"I breaked the spade"; "Look at the mouses"

EMOTIONAL AND SOCIAL DEVELOPMENT

Emotional and social development are closely linked. Emotional development refers to the way we learn to understand our own and other people's emotions. Social development is the way in which we interact with other people, how we form friendships and personal ties with our family members. Good social and emotional development begins in infancy, with a strong **attachment** to a carer; this ideally results in a balanced and happy individual.

NATURE / NURTURE DEBATE

There is divided opinion about whether certain skills or abilities are down to **nature** (**genes** inherited from one's parents: these are unchangeable) or **nurture** (experience since birth: we can control some aspects of this). But there are some traits that are fairly obviously nature or nurture:

Nature	Both / Debatable	Nurture
◆ Facial features	◆ Life expectancy	◆ Hobbies
◆ Eye & hair colour	◆ Weight	◆ Culture
◆ Inherited diseases	◆ Introvert / extrovert	◆ First language
◆ Height	◆ Intelligence	◆ Habits
◆ Race	◆ Sporting ability	◆ Lifestyle

Be careful!

Most "discuss" questions about nature and nurture will focus on things which probably result from both nature and nurture put together. Make sure you provide a balanced argument. **!**

LIFE EXPECTANCY

Life expectancy is the amount of time you can expect to live for: this changes based on your **lifestyle**, social **class** and the country in which you live. For babies born in the UK in 2003, life expectancy is around 77 years old for males, and around 81 years old for females.

Life expectancy has been steadily increasing over the past century. In 1900, life expectancy in the UK was around 45 for men, and 48 for women. The increase in life expectancy is probably due to a combination of having a free National Health Service (NHS), as well as **State Benefits**. Also, houses are now warmer, cleaner, drier and less crowded than they used to be.

INFANCY

Infancy is the life stage between birth and two years old.

GESTATION

Gestation is the nine-month period during which the baby grows in the womb. Clearly, a great deal of growth occurs during this time: the baby grows from being just a fertilised egg, to having many millions of cells. During early gestation, the head, brain and central nervous system grow the quickest; limbs and organs come later.

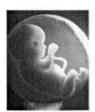 It is still unclear just how much development occurs during gestation. Some physical development must occur, enabling the newborn to suck, swallow, grasp and so on. Intellectual, social and emotional development seem fairly negligible at birth, but there is certainly the potential for development to take place after birth.

INNATE REFLEXES

Newborn babies have several **innate reflexes** (also known as primitive reflexes); these are abilities which they automatically possess at birth. Most of these reflexes seem necessary in order to allow the baby to feed, move and survive during its infancy. (Crying is certainly an ability / instinct which newborn babies possess, but it is not usually classed as a reflex.)

Reflex	Description
Moro / Startle	When startled, a newborn baby throws out its arms and legs, then pulls them back in again and grimaces
Protective	If you place a cloth over a newborn baby's face, he will turn his head to the side and pull away the cloth with his hands
Grasping	A newborn baby will grasp an object placed in his hand (a similar "grasping" action can be seen with the toes, if you stroke the sole of the baby's foot)
Hand-to-mouth	A newborn baby will bring an object to his mouth and begin to suck it
Rooting	When you touch a newborn baby's cheek, he will turn his head in the direction of the touch. This reflex helps the baby find his mother's nipple

Crawling	A newborn baby hovered face down near a surface will show crawling movements
Stepping	If you hold a newborn baby upright with his feet touching the ground, he will make stepping movements

Be careful!
Newborn babies can only grasp an object that is placed into their hand. They will be several months old before they can reach for an object and grasp it.

PHYSICAL DEVELOPMENT

The direction of an infant's physical development is downwards and outwards. This means that babies first gain control of their head and trunk, then the arms and legs, followed by hands and feet, and last of all, precise movements of the fingers. So infants are capable of **gross motor skills** before they are capable of **fine motor skills**.

Gross motor skills

These involve the large muscles in the body. Here are some examples of gross motor skills seen in infancy (in the order they occur):

1. Turning head
2. Rolling over
3. Kicking
4. Leaning forwards
5. Sitting up
6. Crawling
7. Standing up
8. Climbing onto furniture
9. Walking
10. Jumping
11. Running
12. Kicking a ball

Locomotor skills are skills for getting about, such as crawling, walking and running. All locomotor skills are gross motor skills. But there are some gross motor skills such as kicking a ball and sitting up, which do not help you to get about: these are called **non-locomotor skills**.

Be careful!
Locomotor skills are sometimes called locomotive skills. Both these words mean the same thing.

Fine motor skills

Fine motor skills (which are also known as **manipulative skills**) involve the small muscles of the body, particularly the hands and fingers. Here are some examples of fine motor skills seen in infancy (in the order they occur):

1. *Grasping an object in palm*
2. *Inspecting object with finger*
3. *Grasping using "pincer" grip*
4. *Releasing / dropping an object*
5. *Building a small tower of bricks*
6. *Taking off shoes*
7. *Holding a pencil to scribble*
8. *Turning door knobs*
9. *Eating using a spoon*
10. *Scribbling circular shapes*

Bowel and bladder control

With regard to bowel and bladder control, by about 2 years old, a child will probably be dry during most of the day and will be potty training. Complete bladder and bowel control may not be achieved until 4 or 5 years old – particularly bladder control at night time.

INTELLECTUAL DEVELOPMENT

A lot of intellectual development occurs through repetition, **conditioning** and **modelling**. Babies observe and take in everything that is going on around them, and will learn to imitate what they see and hear. Infants enjoy toys with bright colours, flashing lights, and those which make noises and play tunes. They copy what is said and done by adults and other children, and are curious about the world around them.

Language development

An important part of intellectual development for infants is language development. Children will say their first words at around 10 months old, but they will understand many more words. At 12 months old, a child will use around 5 words, and by two years old, may use as many as 200 words.

SOCIAL AND EMOTIONAL DEVELOPMENT

Social and emotional development during infancy mostly occurs through **socialisation** (mixing with other people). Some limited learning will also take place through watching television or hearing stories. A child who is on his own for much of the time and does not get to interact with other children or adults will be poorly socialised, and may develop behavioural or emotional problems.

By the age of 6 months, babies will smile, laugh and enjoy being played with, but may fear strangers. At 9 to 12 months, infants will enjoy playing simple games such as pat-a-cake and peek-a-boo. By 18 months, the infant has a far stronger feeling of being an individual, and will show a range of emotions. Infants will feel confident to explore the environment when a familiar adult is nearby, but may become fearful or upset when in unfamiliar situations.

Attachment

An **attachment** is a strong emotional bond which babies form with a carer (often, the mother or father.) This occurs early on, and even babies who are quite young appear to be soothed more easily by one person in particular. Forming an attachment seems almost instinctive.

Three types of attachment have been observed in infants:

▪ Indiscriminate attachment:	0 – 6 months	*The baby quickly attaches to anyone who is there at the time*
▪ Specific attachment:	7 – 12 months	*The baby attaches to parents or carers and fears strangers*
▪ Multiple attachment:	12 months +	*The baby attaches to close relatives and regular visitors*

Failure to form an initial attachment to someone by the age of 12 months can have a very negative effect on the rest of a person's life. Those who form poor attachments are more at risk of living a **dysfunctional** life. This includes things like: being bullied; being a 'loner'; poor school performance; becoming involved in crime, drugs, or prostitution; being unemployed; having destructive relationships; not forming attachments with their own children; getting divorced; self-harming and/or committing suicide; and suffering a premature death.

PLAY

At first, babies only 'play' on their own and are **egocentric**, meaning that they are oblivious to what other children / babies are doing around them. By the age of 2, infants take part in **parallel play**, where they may imitate adults or older children. **Associative play** occurs next, and this is where infants will play alongside one another and take an interest in what each other is doing – but still they do not really play *with* each other. At around the age of 3, children will engage in pretend play and **co-operative play**, where they actually play *with* other children and can form basic friendships.

CHILDHOOD

Childhood is the life stage between 2 and 8 years old.

PLAY
Play is a vital part of children's development, as it helps them to:

- Become sociable
- Explore their environment
- Improve concentration
- Develop creativity
- Learn new skills
- Develop language
- Solve problems
- Develop memory
- Develop empathy
- Make decisions
- Take responsibility
- Learn intellectually

GROWTH
Children continue to grow at a steady rate during childhood, with boys usually being slightly taller than girls of the same age.

PHYSICAL DEVELOPMENT
Between the ages of 2 and 8, children develop many gross and fine motor skills, through practice and repetition:

* **Gross motor skills:** riding a bike, getting dressed, ball games, swimming, skipping, catching, etc.
* **Fine motor skills:** writing, sewing, drawing / painting, using cutlery, typing, playing video games, etc.

Children will become specialised in their choice of skills (e.g. football, gymnastics, tap dancing, karate.)

Co-ordination
Most skills used in childhood and beyond involve co-ordination. E.g.

- <u>hand-eye co-ordination</u> (for video games, drawing, writing, throwing)
- <u>foot-eye co-ordination</u> (for football, karate, running, going up stairs)
- <u>arm-leg co-ordination</u> (for swimming, dancing, aerobics, running)
- <u>gross-fine co-ordination</u> (for throwing, catching, using cutlery)
- <u>whole body co-ordination</u> (for dancing, gymnastics, getting dressed)

Balance also improves drastically during childhood, and it becomes far less common for children to fall over simply because they lost their balance. By the age of 8 most children will be able to perform almost as many complex operations as adults can.

INTELLECTUAL DEVELOPMENT

A great deal of intellectual and language development occurs during early childhood. Before the age of 5, most children will have learnt:-

- Colours
- Animals
- Foods
- Textures
- Shapes
- Vehicles
- Body parts
- The alphabet
- Counting to 100
- Household objects
- Months of the year
- Days of the week

At the age of 5, a child will experience **gender constancy** – they will know what sex they are, and that it will not change. By the age of 6, children will be learning to read and write, and will be able to do simple addition and subtraction. Intellectual development will continue in all areas throughout childhood, as children will learn history, geography, science, art, religion, music and possibly a foreign language.

Language development

By the age of 4 years old, most children can be understood by strangers. They will form sentences of 4 or more words which are grammatically correct, and they are able to use future and past tenses correctly. By the age of 5 to 6, a child will have a vocabulary of around 5,000 words and will understand almost everything that is said around them in everyday life.

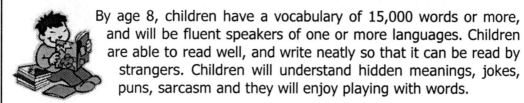

By age 8, children have a vocabulary of 15,000 words or more, and will be fluent speakers of one or more languages. Children are able to read well, and write neatly so that it can be read by strangers. Children will understand hidden meanings, jokes, puns, sarcasm and they will enjoy playing with words.

SOCIAL AND EMOTIONAL DEVELOPMENT

Throughout childhood, children learn to socialise with more and more people, and will learn about themselves and others. By the age of 3, many children attend nursery and so experience separation from their parents for the first time. They will learn how to engage in **co-operative play** and will enjoy spending time with other children.

By the age of 7, friendships are usually sex-segregated. Boys tend to have large, loose friendship groups, with activities centred around fighting, and competitive physical sports such as football. Girls, however, tend to form closer and more intense friendships in pairs or threes, centred around pretend play and co-operative games such as mummies and daddies.

During childhood, all children will develop a strong sense of identity, including any culture or religion.

COMBINED DEVELOPMENT

Many activities learned during childhood require a combination of physical intellectual, social and emotional skills. Some examples are:

Task	Physical	Intellectual	Social / emotional
Playing football	Running, kicking	Understanding the rules	Getting on with other team members
Starting school	Walking, dressing, drawing, writing	Spelling, maths, learning songs or games	Making friends, monitoring own behaviour, being obedient
Having a party	Dancing, playing	Understanding the rules	Getting on with others, turn-taking, sharing
Going out for a meal	Using cutlery	Choosing food, reading the menu	Manners, talking to family
Getting a pet dog	Walking and grooming the dog	Training it to sit, learning about dogs	Praising and getting along with the dog, learning responsibility
Going on holiday	Swimming, playing	Learning a new language	Getting on with siblings, behaviour

SELF-CONCEPT

During childhood, children build up a **self concept**: the idea they have of themselves. This includes how they look, their personality, strengths and weaknesses, their family, religion, age, culture and so on. A child's self-concept will be affected by other people's reactions towards them, and by comparing themselves with other children. One's self-concept changes throughout their life course, and it tends to follow this general pattern:

- <u>Age 2:</u>   An infant will know their name and probably their gender, but not a great deal else about themselves
- <u>Age 6:</u>   A child will be able to give a good physical description of themselves, and they will know their interests. They will also be able to say a few things about their family and friends
- <u>Age 10:</u> A child will have a clear self-image, and can give a full description of themselves, including physical traits and their personality. They will probably be aware of how they compare with other children (e.g. whether they are good at running, writing, maths, etc.)
- <u>Age 17:</u> An adolescent will of course be able to describe themselves physically, but they will probably choose to focus on their personality traits, and activities they enjoy. They will give a more rounded view of themselves, including both their strengths and weaknesses, and any ambitions or future plans
- <u>Adult:</u>   An adult can obviously describe what they look like, but they will probably not see their looks as a major part of their self-image. They'll probably define themselves in terms of what they do for a living, and will mention any children or long-term relationships
- <u>Older person:</u>   An older person's self-concept will be backward-looking: they'll describe what they *used* to do for a living, and the things they liked when they were younger. Children and grandchildren will almost certainly be mentioned.

Modelling

Children learn many skills through **modelling**: copying the behaviour of adults and other children. A lot of social and emotional development occurs in this way, but children can also learn a few physical, intellectual and language skills through modelling. Behaviour learnt through modelling can be good or bad:

<u>Good behaviours:</u>   manners, accents, tidiness, hygiene, religions, turn-taking, sharing, queueing, etc.

<u>Bad behaviours:</u>   swearing, spitting, nose-picking, rudeness, untidiness, racism, cruelty, violence, etc.

> *Be careful!*
> *Modelling is a fairly unconscious process. You don't – for example – learn how to write through modelling, because you have to think hard to learn how to write. Modelling happens with very little effort.*

ADOLESCENCE

Adolescence is the life stage between 9 and 18 years old.

GROWTH AND PHYSICAL DEVELOPMENT

Adolescents continue to grow in height and weight and will achieve their full height during this life stage. Motor skills improve further, and individuals become increasingly specialised in their skills – e.g. judo, tennis, basketball, ballet dancing, lacrosse, etc. But the main physical changes that occur during adolescence centre around puberty.

Puberty

Puberty is the period when **secondary sexual characteristics** develop, and individuals become capable of sexual reproduction. The onset of puberty triggers a growth spurt in girls aged 11 – 12, and boys aged 13 – 15. During puberty, someone's body goes through many changes and their reproductive system becomes functional.

Puberty is triggered by **hormones** (body chemicals): **testosterone** in boys, and **oestrogen** in girls.

Whilst pre-pubescent boys and girls have similar body shapes, during puberty, the body changes so that girls become wider at the hips and chest, giving them a narrower waist and hourglass shape, whereas boys get broader shoulders, giving their torso a 'triangular' shape.

Sexual characteristics

Sexual characteristics are things that make someone male or female, as well as some sexual traits that arise during puberty, such as body hair. Sexual characteristics are either primary or secondary.

- **Primary sexual characteristics** are sexual characteristics which have been there since birth.

- **Secondary sexual characteristics** are those which develop or change during puberty.

Male sexual characteristics		
Primary	**Secondary**	
▪ Penis	▪ Pubic hair	▪ Voice breaks
▪ Testicles	▪ Sperm production begins	▪ Chest hair
▪ Scrotum	▪ Armpit (**axillary**) hair	▪ Erections
	▪ Facial hair	▪ Penis and testicles enlarge
	▪ Shoulders broaden	▪ Ejaculation (**wet dreams**)
	▪ Muscles develop	▪ Body hair (arms, legs etc.)

Female sexual characteristics		
Primary	**Secondary**	
▪ Vagina	▪ Pubic hair	▪ Menstruation begins (**menarche**)
▪ Uterus	▪ Ovulation begins	▪ Armpit (**axillary**) hair
▪ Clitoris	▪ Breasts develop	▪ Leg / arm hair increases slightly
▪ Ovaries	▪ Voice pitch drops	▪ Fat deposits give curvy shape
	▪ Pelvis widens	▪ Vagina, womb and clitoris enlarge

By age 17 to 18, virtually all males and females will be fully grown and fully sexually developed.

Hormones

Hormones are released throughout one's life, but during adolescence, their functions are most noticeable. The release of hormones will affect an adolescent's physical, intellectual, social and emotional development.

The hypothalamus and pituitary gland (in the brain) control and stimulate the release of hormones elsewhere in the body. Growth-related hormones are released in both boys and girls: these cause growth spurts. **Gonadotropic hormones** are those related to sexual development. These are released from the testes in boys, and from the ovaries in girls.

♦ **Oestrogen** and **progesterone** in girls stimulate the menstrual cycle, production of eggs and the development of other secondary sexual characteristics
♦ **Testosterone** in boys is responsible for the growth spurt, pubic hair, facial changes, sperm production and the other secondary sexual characteristics

Hormones are responsible for the physical changes seen in adolescents, as well as their sexual desires, desire for independence and their new-found thinking abilities.

INTELLECTUAL DEVELOPMENT

Adolescents become increasingly able to think in complicated ways which were impossible during childhood: they develop **abstract thinking** skills. Abstract thinking skills include the following:

- <u>Thinking hypothetically:</u> adolescents are able to think about possible situations or options that could be open to them
- <u>Planning ahead:</u> adolescents can think ahead about what things they will need, e.g. for a holiday
- <u>Metacognition:</u> adolescents can think about the way in which they think and reason things through
- <u>Second-order thinking:</u> adolescents can hold two lots of information at once, e.g. knowing which rules 'outrank' other rules, and applying information sensibly in new situations
- <u>Rhetorical questions:</u> adolescents can think about life's 'big questions' about politics, religion, morality, life etc.
- **<u>Decentring</u>:** adolescents can see things from other people's point of view: they are no longer **egocentric**

Formal operational

Jean Piaget (see p22-23) said that adolescents can think logically without any concrete objects to handle or look at: children cannot do this. For example, a person of 12 years or older would be able to work out the following problem in their head; a child of 7 to 11 years of age would be able to work it out if he or she could draw a diagram; and a child under seven might not be able to work it out at all.

▶ *Graham is taller than John, and Philip is shorter than John but taller than Mike. Who is tallest?*

Language Development

Language development continues right through adolescence, with individuals becoming increasingly fluent and articulate. This is improved by schooling, social engagements, reading, the internet, television and many other situations.

Education and Jobs

Many adolescents will continue their education beyond GCSEs, to do A-Levels or vocational qualifications, followed by university. Clearly, this type of education will facilitate adolescents' intellectual development. But those who leave education are also likely to develop intellectually through their jobs or training programmes.

SOCIAL AND EMOTIONAL DEVELOPMENT

Adolescents' social and emotional development involves moving away from family relationships, in favour of friendships or boyfriend / girlfriend relationships.

Peer pressure

Peer pressure can be a very strong force, and adolescents may feel pushed into doing things which they are unsure about, such as smoking, having sex, taking drugs, or committing crime.

A teenager's **self-concept** can be very fragile, and adolescents like to feel accepted by their peers. They may feel self-conscious about their appearance or physical development, and there is increasing pressure for adolescents to enter into sexual relationships. It is usually during this life stage that people realise their sexual orientation, or they may wish to 'experiment' sexually.

Independence

Adolescence is a time when individuals tend to break away from the confines of their family and strive for independence. It is normal for adolescents and their parents to disagree or argue about how much independence a teen should have. Some common issues that adolescents and their parents fall out about are:

- Dress sense
- Curfews
- Dietary choices
- Smoking / alcohol / drugs
- Social activities
- Money
- Friendship groups or gangs
- Sexual relationships
- Schooling and further education
- Morals and values
- Tidiness and housework
- Career choices / unemployment

Many people will move out of the family home during adolescence; they may move to a different town to attend a university, or they may find that steady employment means they can afford their own house.

ADULTHOOD

Adulthood is the life stage from 19 years onwards.

Adulthood can be separated into **Early adulthood** (19 to 45 years), **Middle adulthood** (45 to 65 years) and **Later adulthood / Old age** (from 65 years onwards). The information in this section concerns adults from 19 to 65 years of age.

PHYSICAL DEVELOPMENT

Most adults will have reached their full height by the age of 19, and will not alter in height during adulthood. Weight, however, can change drastically depending on someone's **lifestyle** (see p55-59)

Adults will see an increase in speed, agility and strength up until the age of approximately 24 to 26 years of age, after which, a gradual decline in abilities is likely to be observed. However, most people are capable of learning new gross and fine motor skills throughout adulthood.

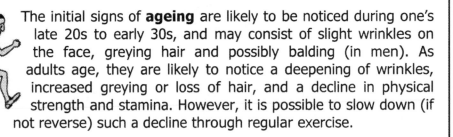 The initial signs of **ageing** are likely to be noticed during one's late 20s to early 30s, and may consist of slight wrinkles on the face, greying hair and possibly balding (in men). As adults age, they are likely to notice a deepening of wrinkles, increased greying or loss of hair, and a decline in physical strength and stamina. However, it is possible to slow down (if not reverse) such a decline through regular exercise.

Women go through the **menopause** at around age 45 to 55. This is when the reproductive system shuts down, and a woman is no longer capable of bearing children. There is still some debate about whether a male menopause exists!

INTELLECTUAL DEVELOPMENT

Adults tend to develop their intellectual skills throughout their lives, either through formal schooling, jobs, or other pursuits. Language development and articulacy often improves further, and some adults may take up a foreign language.

Skills which are not used a great deal will diminish – for example, complex mathematical abilities, or other subjects learned in school. Many adults choose to have children; an experience which requires a great deal of learning and development of new intellectual skills.

Be careful!
Intellectual development is never complete. Most adults are capable of learning new intellectual skills throughout their entire lives.

SOCIAL AND EMOTIONAL DEVELOPMENT

One's relationships with others change throughout adulthood: people move from being children, to husbands and wives, through to parents and possibly grandparents.

Leaving home and finding a partner are typical things that a person in their 20s will do. People tend to choose someone who has equivalent values, looks, and intellectual abilities as themselves. Some relationships will lead to marriage and/or children. Becoming a parent is a life-changing step, which most people find rewarding and purposeful. However, if people take on too much, they can suffer from **role strain**, where they have too many demands to cope with.

Getting promoted is a common feature of people's working lives; this can bring greater satisfaction and income, but also greater stress and demands on people's time and intellectual abilities.

Death of one's parents is unfortunately something which most people experience during adulthood – and possibly the loss of other family members, friends, colleagues, or their spouse.

Adults' attitudes or relationships change continually throughout their lives, as they grow and learn and experience new things.

LATER ADULTHOOD

Later adulthood (old age) is the life stage from 65 years onwards.

PHYSICAL DEVELOPMENT

Generally speaking, there is little physical improvement seen during later adulthood, though regular exercise and health care throughout adulthood can slow down many of the effects of ageing. Some of the most noticeable physical effects of ageing are:

- <u>Skin:</u> Loses elasticity and becomes thinner: older people have wrinkled skin on their faces and hands
- <u>Hair:</u> Hair usually loses its pigment and goes grey; men (and some women) may experience balding
- <u>Reproductive system:</u> In women, this will have shut down at around age 50, but men may continue to produce sperm until decades later, although impotency can become a problem after age 65
- <u>Senses:</u> Hearing and eyesight often decline with age, but can be corrected by hearing aids or glasses
- <u>Muscles:</u> Arm, leg and other muscles weaken; elderly people have less strength and stamina
- <u>Bones:</u> Bones become more thin and brittle (osteoporosis)
- <u>Joints:</u> Joints often become stiffer and/or more painful; people lose mobility and suppleness
- <u>Height:</u> Some shrinkage occurs due to disc compression, and older people may appear hunched
- <u>Heat control:</u> Older people are more at risk of illness / death due to heat-waves or cold winters
- <u>Immunity to illness:</u> It is harder for older people to fight off illnesses such as flu and pneumonia
- <u>Organs:</u> Older people are more likely to suffer from many forms of cancer, heart disease, heart attacks, angina and organ failure, but some of this is related to lifestyle (see p55-59)
- <u>Balance:</u> Balance deteriorates, so older people are more likely to fall over
- <u>Blood pressure:</u> Rises with age, bringing greater risk of stroke
- <u>Hormones:</u> Reduced hormone production causes lower metabolism, and possibly diabetes (after the **menopause**, women produce less oestrogen, so the small amounts of testosterone in their bodies can make them appear more masculine; they may experience balding on the head, and growth of facial hair)

INTELLECTUAL DEVELOPMENT

The brain decreases in size and weight during later adulthood, which is often reflected in some loss of mental ability. However, many older people are capable of learning new skills and abilities, so old age is not necessarily about mental decline.

Undoubtedly, skills that were learned early on in life and are practised regularly such as talking, reading and mental arithmetic are far more likely to be retained than skills that are never used or were learned later in life. Some older people may have trouble remembering what happened yesterday, but retain very clear memories of their early childhood or adult life.

Dementia

Old age – particularly very old age (80 and over) – is often accompanied by severe mental decline: this could be down to **dementia** or **Alzheimer's disease**. These can have the effect of a severe mental illness, with patients becoming distressed, confused, forgetful, violent or detached. Such conditions will not improve, and can often result in the older person needing special care, either by moving in with their children, or by moving in to a nursing home or other residential care.

SOCIAL AND EMOTIONAL DEVELOPMENT

Unless the older person has dementia or Alzheimer's disease, a decline in social and emotional skills is rare. However, older people do witness a decline in the number of **social roles** they have (they used to be a mother, daughter, sister, colleague and carer; now they are just a mother and grandmother).

Retirement can bring about a new lease of life for some people who decide to travel, write a novel, paint, etc. Increased time with one's spouse can lead to happiness and greater fulfilment; however sometimes, it puts increased strain on the relationship, which can lead to unhappiness or separation.

Death is an inevitable part of old age, and the death of a spouse, friends and relatives can leave an elderly person socially isolated and emotionally vulnerable.

NORMS

A developmental **norm** is an average expected milestone that should be seen in most people at a certain age. The table below shows the expected norms during an average **life span**.

Age	Physical	Intellectual	Social & Emotional
0 – 2 months	Innate reflexes: startle; protective; gripping; sucking; rooting; crawling; stepping		Cries when cold, wet nappy, feeling hungry or uncomfortable; recognises mother's smell and voice and is soothed by it
2 – 4 months	Lifts head when lying face down; holds things placed in hands; turns head towards sounds		Watches parent or carer's face; smiles and coos; enjoys being handled and cuddled
4 – 6 months	Reaches for and grasps objects	Babbles short sounds, e.g. 'da… da'	Forms quick attachment to anyone; laughs and enjoys being played with
6 – 9 months	Sits unaided; rolls over; transfers object from one hand to the other	Understands some words; uses noises and gestures, experiences **object permanence**	Forms attachment with parents / carers; fears strangers
9 – 12 months	Crawls; is learning to walk	Babbles repetitive sounds, e.g. 'dadadadada'; babbling becomes more varied; at 10 months, understands 15 to 20 words; at 12 months can say 2 to 6 words, and can understand dozens more	Forms attachment with relatives and regular visitors; discriminates between strangers and familiar adults; plays peek-a-boo

Age	Physical	Intellectual	Social & Emotional
12–18 months	Walks unaided; climbs stairs; kneels down; takes off shoes; stacks 2 blocks	Knows parts of the body; uses **holophrases** (when the same word with different intonations is used to mean different things, e.g. 'cat' means 'Look at the cat' or 'Where is the cat?'); says around 20 words the carer can understand	Is affectionate towards family and carers; begins to explore environment if familiar adult is nearby; uses words to communicate with family; has a stronger feeling of being an individual
18–24 months	Walks well and runs; pushes / pulls toys on wheels; stacks blocks; jumps with both feet	Uses **telegraphic speech**, (two-word sentences used in a grammatical way: 'daddy come', 'kick ball'); by 2 years, uses about 200 words; knows what sex they are; scribbles with pens; identifies pictures (e.g. a duck)	Points to objects to show familiar adults; explores environment and shows increased independence; shows strong emotions, e.g. anger, joy, excitement
2 – 3 years	Runs easily; climbs onto furniture on own; picks up objects without falling over; throws a ball; turns door knobs	Uses plurals; still makes **virtuous errors**, e.g. 'sheeps' 'drawed'; joins up short sentences using 'and'; learns by imitating others; completes a three-piece puzzle; matches textures; matches colours; knows big and little	Is learning to understand others; is interested in other children; plays by imitating others **(parallel play)**; begins to talk when playing (pretend play); plays alongside others (**associative play**)
3 – 4 years	Walks up stairs with one foot per step; pedals and steers a trike; catches a large ball; holds a pencil normally; gets dressed	Knows light and heavy, and long and short; can repeat a simple story; matches into pairs; sorts simple objects; knows a few colours; knows three shapes; counts to ten; uses future and past tenses appropriately	Plays with other children (**co-operative play**); begins to realise the value of sharing, turn-taking and friendships

Age	Physical	Intellectual	Soc & Emo
4 – 5 years	Walks up and down stairs with one foot per step; uses a bat and ball; kicks a ball; builds recognisable models with bricks; draws recognisable pictures; may be able to write a little	Can find a number of objects (e.g. four cubes); names five textures; knows times of day (bedtime; dinnertime); knows eight colours; matches symbols; counts to twenty. By 5 years old, vocabulary is about 5,000 words or more	Understands that if mum goes away, the relationship still exists and she will return
5 – 6 years	Plays ball games well; skips with a rope; excellent motor control to thread a needle and sew simple stitches; has complete control over bowel and bladder	Knows their gender is fixed (**gender constancy**); accurately counts 20 items; writes own name; arranges objects in order of size; knows days of the week and months of the year; is learning to read; counts up to 100	Chooses to spend time with some friends more than others
7 – 12 years	Children continue to grow and improve motor skills, and can learn specialised sports (ballet, hockey, cricket, athletics)	Articulacy and cognitive abilities develop well through schooling; by 8 years old, vocabulary is up to 15,000 words or more; they are fluent speakers of their language	Friendships become increasingly important, and might begin to supersede family ties
12 – 16 years	Puberty begins: (Boys: voice lowers; pubic hair grows; facial hair begins to grow; sperm production begins; shoulders become more broad) (Girls: menstruation begins; breasts develop; pubic hair grows; pelvis widens)	Individuals may leave compulsory education; cognitive skills and language skills are increasing through schooling and hobbies; there is a marked difference in the intellects of people	Friendships are probably more important than relationships with family; peer pressure to conform can be high; non-acceptance of peers can cause bullying or depression

Age	Physical	Intellectual	Social & Emotional
17 – 30 years	In men, hair growth may continue to increase on face and chest, and maybe on the back; both males and females might continue to increase in weight	Many people continue into further and higher education. Those who get jobs are also likely to learn new skills and abilities	Individuals usually become sexually active during this period; relationships are formed with both sexes in a stable way, and supersede family ties, individuals may have children
30 – 45 years	Physical signs of ageing begin: greying hair; wrinkles	New skills continue to be learned and developed	Many couples have children and enjoy looking after them; it is both challenging and rewarding
45 – 60 years	Menopause occurs (in women); hair goes grey; wrinkles are more pronounced	New skills continue to be learned and developed	One's children may grow up and leave home; leaving more time for marital relationships
60 – 75 years	Physical abilities are in decline, though many people still live active lives. Bones may become more brittle; joints ache	Most people still have active minds and learn new skills during retirement	Most people retire during this life stage; family relationships are more important, as parents have died; friends, siblings or partners may begin to die
75 + years	Physical abilities decline further; death is not unexpected during this period	The brain is still capable of learning new skills; keeping the mind active can help prevent further deterioration; senile dementia or Alzheimer's disease may develop	Some individuals may move into care homes, or move in with younger family members for additional help

NATURE AND NURTURE

- **Nature** is what you've inherited genetically – you can't control this.
- **Nurture** is your lifestyle, social situation and life experience: you can control these things to a certain extent

The nature / nurture debate is about whether certain physical, personality or lifestyle traits are due to a person's **genes** (**nature**), or to their upbringing (**nurture**). Whilst a whole person is the result of both nature and nurture working simultaneously, some aspects of growth and development are mostly down to nature, whilst others are more affected by nurture.

GROWTH
Nature
Growth (in height) is wholly genetic: there are hardly any social, lifestyle or environmental factors that affect someone's height. (Only if a child is continually starved over several years will their growth in height be slower than expected.)

Nurture
Growth in weight is very much dependent upon someone's lifestyle: the food they eat and the exercise they do (or don't do). Whilst there *might* be a genetic predisposition to putting on weight easily, this can almost always be controlled by a sensible diet and exercise.

PHYSICAL DEVELOPMENT
Nature
One's physical development is very much dependent on genetics. **Maturation** is a person's genetically pre-programmed body clock: it tells the body when to start puberty, when to start ageing and possibly when to die. Much of this is passed on genetically, so a man in a family with a history of baldness should expect to go bald, and someone with a family history of longevity (living long) can possibly expect to also live a long time.

A person's looks are wholly dependent on genes; their skin colour, face shape, etc. To a certain extent, their physical abilities are also dependent on genes, such as the age they'll walk at, or whether they'll be a fast runner. There is a genetic predisposition towards some illnesses, such as heart disease and some cancers.

Nurture

Someone's health and fitness is dependent upon what they eat and how much they exercise. Things like smoking, drinking alcohol, eating badly and doing little exercise all increase the likelihood of getting certain illnesses, which can affect physical development.

INTELLECTUAL DEVELOPMENT

Nature

Some people may be predisposed to being good at maths, or art, but this would have to be developed and worked at during one's life. It is often the case that intelligent parents have intelligent children, but whether that is down to genetics or upbringing is not always clear. Nature and nurture seem to have to 'work together' to produce a person who is good at something.

Nurture

The language we learn to speak is entirely non-genetic: a Chinese baby brought up in France will speak French, and a French baby brought up in China will speak Chinese. Accents and vocabulary are learned through hearing and copying speech patterns. However, it seems clear that we do have a genetically pre-programmed *ability* to pick up whatever language we hear around us.

SOCIAL AND EMOTIONAL DEVELOPMENT

Nature

It's *possible* that someone may have a predisposition towards certain personality traits, such at being extrovert, suffering from depression or having an 'addictive personality'. However, none of these have been proven.

Nurture

Almost all social and emotional development is probably down to nurture rather than nature. People learn how to socialise and get on with others by watching and imitating other people. Without experience, it is unlikely that anyone would have any idea about social norms or customs, or how to form relationships.

> ### Be careful!
> *Most developmental traits (but not growth) are down to both nature and nurture – make sure you give a balanced argument.*

GENETIC INFLUENCES

Your genetic makeup is completely inherited, with half of your genes coming from your mother, and half from your father.

GENES

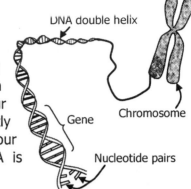

A **gene** is a short section of **DNA** (deoxyribo-nucleic acid) which has a particular purpose (e.g. blue eyes, brown skin); it exists in a double helix (twisted ladder shape). All of your genes are added together to determine exactly how you will look – and possibly some of your intellectual or personality traits as well. DNA is coiled up into X-shaped **chromosomes**.

DNA double helix
Chromosome
Gene
Nucleotide pairs

Chromosomes exist in pairs, and are in the nucleus of every living cell. Humans have 46 chromosomes (23 pairs) in every cell except egg and sperm cells (**gametes**). Egg and sperm cells have 23 *single* chromosomes, ready to be paired up during conception.

The 'rungs' of the double helix DNA ladder are made up of four **nucleotide** bases (chemicals):

- Adenine (A) - Thymine (T) - Guanine (G) - Cytosine (C)

To reproduce itself, the DNA unravels itself, splits apart, and the nucleotides each bond with new partners. The fact that adenine only bonds with thymine (A – T) and guanine bonds only with cytosine (G – C) means that the new strands of DNA will be identical to the previous strands.

HOW SEX IS CHOSEN

There are two types of sex chromosome: **X** and **Y**. Females have two **X** chromosomes, whereas males have one **X** and one **Y**. Because eggs and sperm only contain half the information needed to make a baby, each contains just one sex chromosome. The egg will always

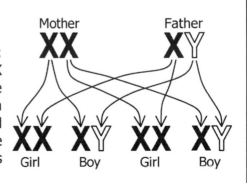

Mother Father
XX **XY**

XX **XY** **XX** **XY**
Girl Boy Girl Boy

contain an **X** chromosome (because the mother only has **X** chromosomes to pass on) but the sperm may contain either an **X** or a **Y** chromosome (as the father has both types of chromosome to pass on), so the sperm determines the sex of the baby.

Each baby will get one sex chromosome off the mother, and one off the father. As the diagram shows, there is an equal chance of it being either a boy or a girl. Other hereditary information is passed on in a similar (but more complex) way.

		Mother	
Fig 1.1		X	X
Father	X	XX	XX
	Y	XY	XY

DOMINANT AND RECESSIVE GENES

Genes can be either **dominant** or **recessive**. When there is one dominant gene and one recessive, the dominant one takes over and the recessive one is not seen. Only when someone has two recessive genes is the trait seen. Things such as having blue eyes, attached earlobes, or a long second toe are carried on recessive genes, so only if someone has two genes for blue eyes will they actually *have* blue eyes. If they have one gene for blue eyes and one for brown eyes, the dominant brown-eye gene takes over and the person has brown eyes. The same system applies for other genetically inherited traits.

		Mother	
Fig 1.2		Br	Bl
Father	Br	BrBr	BrBl
	Bl	BlBr	BlBl

As with sex, a simple way to work out the chances of dominant or recessive genes being passed on is to draw a table with the mother's and father's genes on it, and then fill in the children's possible gene combinations.

The table above shows the distribution of the genes for brown and blue eyes from a mother and father, and their potential children. It can be seen that although the mother and father both have brown eyes, there's a one in four chance that any child of theirs will have blue eyes.

Be careful!
The chance of having any given trait 'resets' itself for each child. Even if the parents in Fig 1.1 have five sons already, there is still a 50-50 chance that their next child will be a boy. The same goes for eye colour: if the parents in Fig 1.2 already have a child with blue eyes, there's still a 1 in 4 chance that their next child will have blue eyes too.

!

PHYSICAL DEVELOPMENT

Genes have a dramatic effect upon people's physical development. Genes govern one's body clock, and will probably dictate the age at which a person will learn to walk, when they'll go grey, whether they'll be athletic, or whether they will be prone to putting weight on easily. But people will often be able to change their dispositions, depending on what sort of lifestyle they adopt, or what sort of social context they are born into.

Genetic Disorders and Conditions

Down's Syndrome is one of many chromosome disorders; it occurs when a person has 47 chromosomes instead of the normal 46 chromosomes. Down's Syndrome is associated with characteristic physical features (round face, long tongue, almond-shaped eyes), as well as severe learning disabilities. There is no treatment or cure.

There is also evidence that some cancers (e.g. breast cancer) can run in families, so these cancers are thought to be at least partially related to genes. However, most illnesses and disabilities are not genetically inherited, but are a result of social, lifestyle, or environmental factors – or sometimes they are just down to chance.

INTELLECTUAL DEVELOPMENT

It is unclear how much of one's intelligence is down to inherited genes. It certainly seems that some people are naturally 'gifted' and are able to play musical instruments, or paint very good pictures from an exceptionally early age. This seems unlikely to be related to one's upbringing. Mathematical, linguistic or other academic abilities may also be partially related to one's inherited genetic makeup, but as with any genetic predispositions, one must have the chance to practice their talent in order to get really good at it.

SOCIAL AND EMOTIONAL DEVELOPMENT

It seems very unlikely that much social or emotional development is genetically inherited. Some babies cry more than others, for no apparent reason, so this could be partly inherited. Also, some people seem to be extrovert virtually from birth, and so this may be somehow related to their genes. But any of this could be the result of what happened to their mother during pregnancy, so strictly speaking, would be the result of 'experience' rather than inherited genetic makeup.

SOCIAL INFLUENCES

Social factors that affect development are the society in which someone lives, and the social elements of one's life, for example, family, friends, education, religion, class and culture.

FAMILY
Family types
There are several different types of family, but each involves one or more adults and their children:

- **Nuclear family**
- Unmarried family
- Foster family
- Single parent family
- Same-sex family
- Extended family
- Adopted family
- Step family
- Grown-up family

One's family type has an effect on their development, because some types of family may have less money, and so have to live in poorer areas of a town. Children in some types of family (e.g. a same-sex family or foster family) may get bullied by other children, which could affect their **self-concept** and self-esteem.

Unmarried families and single parent families have become much more common over the last 30 years, but there still might be some **social stigma** (negative beliefs) attached to belonging to such a family.

Development
One's family type does not really affect a child's physical or intellectual development a great deal, but it *may* mean that, e.g. the adult in a single-parent family has less time to spend with their children, to play with them physically, or help them with homework.

One's social and emotional development is far more likely to be affected by their family – different families may instil different morals and **values** into their children. The children may associate the family with happiness and stability... or with lack of privacy and strict discipline. This could affect their **self-concept**.

Functions of the Family

The family has many functions or uses in the modern world, but the following are possibly the most important:

- Protection — The family provides protection from danger – e.g. starvation, paedophiles, traffic
- Affection — The family provides love and affection, so its members develop normal, positive **self-concepts**
- Reproductive — Through sexual activity, the family provides the next generation of society
- Socialisation — The family teaches children norms and **values**, about how to act and behave
- Education — The family provides an initial education for children – e.g. learning words, colours, animals, potty training
- Economic — The family provides financially for children – e.g. clothes, food, warmth, a home, toys

> *Be careful!*
> *Children can't choose their families, but they are certainly not 'inherited': only genetic traits are inherited.* **!**

SOCIALISATION

Socialisation is the act of learning how to mix with other people, and how to behave. This can be broken down into primary and secondary:

- **Primary socialisation:** *Takes place first, within the family* – children learn how to act, as well as norms and values
- **Secondary socialisation:** *Takes place after primary socialisation, within schools, playgroups, or when mixing with others* – children learn more how to act in public, with strangers

Proper **socialisation** is vital for one's effective social and emotional development. Children who are not properly socialised (e.g. they were kept from mixing with other children) may not know how to act around others; they may get bullied or have trouble with relationships, or even develop personality disorders and live a **dysfunctional** life of crime, **substance abuse**, or **social exclusion**.

Some things learned through socialisation are:

Manners	Sharing	Friendships	Co-operation
Teamwork	Turn-taking	Empathy	Culture
Religion	Patience	Respect	Kindness

RACE AND ETHNICITY

One's **race** refers to the colour of their skin, and their physical (usually facial) features. **Ethnicity** includes one's race, but also refers to their religion, culture and way of life. In the UK, most people are white-skinned (Caucasian); everyone else belongs to an ethnic minority. Being in an ethnic minority can turn out to be a good thing or a bad thing.

Good things

★ They are more likely to be bilingual or multilingual
★ Asian children often do better in school than their white counterparts (though black children generally do less well)
★ Second- and third-generation immigrants can feel like they fit into two cultures (e.g. Indian culture and English culture)
★ **Positive discrimination** may mean that people from ethnic minorities are more likely to be offered a job than a similarly qualified white person (*this is disputable*)
★ Most people are not at all racist

Bad things

★ They are more likely to suffer racism
★ They live in poorer areas and inner cities
★ Their jobs are more poorly paid
★ They are more likely to be victims of crime
★ Some races (e.g. black African) are more likely to be convicted of a crime
★ They are more likely to suffer **social exclusion** (being seriously disadvantaged with regard to opportunities, and not feeling a part of mainstream society)
★ There may be a language barrier (or a strong accent barrier) when talking with other people

Most of these points concern someone's social and emotional development, rather than their physical and intellectual development. Someone's ethnicity will affect their life chances, self-concept, attitudes and values.

> ### Be careful!
> *Race is genetically inherited, but the <u>effects</u> of belonging to an ethnic minority are socially determined. There is nothing inherently good or bad about any particular race, but people may be treated differently because of **prejudice** or **stereotyping**.*

CLASS

Social class generally refers to someone's wealth, education, socio-economic status or job. There are many different class systems, but one of the most common is the ABC1 system:

GROUP A: <u>Professional workers:</u> Lawyers, doctors, scientists, professors, managers of large organisations

GROUP B: <u>Managerial and technical occupations:</u> Farmers, teachers, white-collar workers, small office managers

GROUP C1: <u>Skilled non-manual:</u> Office workers, civil servants, police and armed forces

GROUP C2: <u>Skilled manual:</u> Electricians, plumbers, builders, joiners, carpenters, nurses

GROUP D : <u>Semi-Skilled Manual:</u> Bus drivers, lorry drivers, shop assistants, hairdressers, butchers, cooks,

GROUP E: <u>Unskilled Manual + others:</u> Labourers, waiters, bin men, retired people, students, unemployed people

Effects of being poor

Social class is something that can affect a person's **life course** enormously, and will govern their opportunities and choices from birth until death. For example, being born into a poor, working class family *might* mean...

- you have poorer quality toys when you are a baby
- you are more likely to attend state education
- you do less well in school
- you find it difficult to go on to further or higher education because of spiralling costs
- you have to take a poorly paid job
- you are less likely to eat well, and more likely to be obese
- you are more likely to smoke or become addicted to drugs
- you have little chance of moving out of poverty
- you have less chance to travel
- you are more likely to be convicted of a crime
- you are more likely to be a victim of crime
- you have worse housing
- you are more likely to get divorced
- you suffer **social exclusion**
- you suffer poverty during retirement
- you may die prematurely[*]

* None of these are certainties, but they do reflect general societal trends

Social mobility

Social mobility is the possibility of someone changing their class (ideally for the better). In the past, it was almost unheard of for someone to change their class and work themselves out of **poverty**: if you were born into a poor family, you'd grow up poor, have poor children, be poor all your life and die poor: this is called the '**circle of deprivation**'. This still happens in many countries in the developing world.

Some people think that Britain is a **meritocracy** – a society where your position in society is determined by individual merit (i.e. your skills and abilities) rather than by what class you were born into – but this is highly debatable. For example, university tuition fees are forcing many poor people to forego higher education and get a job, locking them into a circle of deprivation that is not easy to break.

RELIGION

Religion plays an enormous part in some people's lives, and can affect the friends a person makes, who they marry, what food they will eat, what their interests and hobbies will be, their attitudes and their self-concept.

In the UK, around 70% of people describe themselves as Christian, although many of these people rarely attend church or actively participate in their religion. Twenty-five percent of people in the UK have no religion or are atheists; the remaining five percent of people in the UK are a mixture of Muslim, Hindu, Buddhist, Sikh and Jewish people.

Religious festivals are extremely popular, with families and friends coming together to exchange gifts, eat, drink, worship and socialise. The most widely celebrated religious festival in the UK is Christmas, although this is not always followed in a religious way.

People who are religious can take great comfort in the idea that a loved one who has died still exists in some way, and that there is a god overseeing the world and taking care of humanity. Social and emotional development are greatly affected by religion, and people tend to find friends and a partner who shares their religious beliefs. However, religious differences can also be a source of social tension, hatred and even violence among some people.

LIFESTYLE INFLUENCES

Lifestyle is the way a person chooses to live their life. The term 'lifestyle' can refer to a range of things, but some of the most important aspects of one's lifestyle are:

- Diet
- Exercise
- Health
- Drinking alcohol
- Job
- Smoking
- Drug use
- Hobbies / leisure activities

DIET

Diet is really important because it has drastic effects upon someone's physical and intellectual development – which can in turn affect social and emotional development.

Poverty and nutrition

Poorer people tend to have a worse diet than people in higher classes. Poorer people...

- Spend more money on foods high in fat and sugar, such as chips and sweets
- Spend less on foods rich in nutrients, such as fresh fruit and vegetables
- Tend to eat more processed food, containing high levels of salt, such as microwave meals
- Are statistically more obese than people from higher classes
- On average, have a life expectancy ten years less than their upper class counterparts

A healthy diet

To ensure you are eating a healthy diet, you should...

- Eat more fruit and vegetables, aiming for at least five portions a day. Include fruit at breakfast
- Choose healthy snacks such as fruit, yoghurt, celery, or whole-grain crackers and cheese
- Serve lean meats and other good sources of protein, such as eggs, fish, and nuts; avoid red meats
- Choose wholegrain foods so you get more fibre. i.e. wholemeal bread, brown rice, wholegrain cereals
- Limit fat intake: avoid deep-fried foods: instead, try boiling, grilling, roasting, or steaming foods
- Limit sugar intake from fizzy drinks, sweets, cakes, chocolate and biscuits

- Cut down on salt by eating less processed food such as ready meals, and adding less salt to food
- Limit alcohol intake: drink alcohol only within the recommended limits, and do not binge-drink
- Eat a varied diet: change your shopping list every week to help keep you out of unhealthy food habits
- Eat regular meals: a regular routine helps people control their diet and weight; eat three meals a day and don't skip breakfast
- Control portion sizes so that the amount of energy you consume matches your level of activity

Eating a poor diet is one of the main contributors towards a range of health problems such as:

- High blood pressure
- Respiratory problems
- Multiple organ failure
- Premature births

- Diabetes
- Stroke
- Obesity
- Anaemia

- Osteoporosis
- Heart disease
- Malnutrition
- Heart attacks

EXERCISE

Exercise should go hand in hand with a good diet, the result of which will be a fit body which is not overweight. One should aim to do around half an hour's **cardiovascular** activity three times a week, such as running, cycling, or playing squash.

Exercising and keeping fit can have enormous benefits on a person's life – not just physically, but socially and emotionally as well.

The benefits of exercise

- Helps you maintain a healthy weight
- Increases "good" cholesterol
- Gives you healthier heart and lungs
- Lowers high blood pressure
- Helps maintain healthy blood sugar levels
- Prevents premature ageing
- Improves mood and prevents depression
- Gives you a challenge
- Increases stamina
- Promotes bone density
- You have fun
- You can make new friends
- Makes you feel young
- Give you better muscle tone
- Increases strength
- You look more attractive
- Helps prevent premature deaths due to stroke, diabetes, angina, heart disease, heart attack, obesity, organ failure and so on.

Obesity

Being overweight or **obese** is an increasing problem in the UK and many other developed countries. This is primarily due to people eating a diet which is high in fat and sugar, and not exercising enough. Obesity is defined as having a **Body Mass Index** (BMI) of 30 or more. BMI is calculated by dividing a person's weight in kilograms by their height in metres squared.

BMI	Weight status
Up to 18.5	Underweight
18.5 – 25	Healthy
25 – 30	Overweight
30 – 35	Obese
35 +	Morbidly obese

SMOKING

In the UK in 2005, about 25% of men and 23% of women were smokers. Among secondary school children aged 11 to 15, 10% smoke cigarettes, and nearly a quarter of 15-year-olds are addicted to smoking.

Smoking is very dangerous, and is a major contributing factor towards:
- Lung cancer
- Other cancers
- Heart disease
- Angina
- Strokes
- Mouth cancer
- High blood pressure
- Bronchitis
- Heart attacks
- Emphysema
- Cancer of the larynx
- Narrowed arteries
- Cardiovascular disease
- Respiratory problems
- Asthma

Smoking during pregnancy or around a newborn baby can cause:
- Stillbirths
- **Ectopic pregnancy**
- Cerebral palsy
- Miscarriages
- Placental complications
- Poor quality breast milk
- Low birth weights
- Cleft palate
- Cot death
- (plus increased risk of all the above (asthma, cancers, etc.) after the birth)

Giving up Smoking

There are _no_ health benefits of smoking, aside from a temporary reduction in stress levels. Some of the benefits of giving up are:
- Your blood vessels begin to reopen and your circulation improves
- Your energy levels start to rise as the carbon monoxide leaves your body
- Increased chance of conceiving and having a healthy pregnancy and baby
- Healthier children who are less likely to start smoking
- You no longer put those around you at risk
- You breathe more easily
- Your risk of serious disease starts to fall
- Less chance of starting a house fire

ALCOHOL

Over 90% of Britain's adults drink alcoholic beverages, with well over 50% doing so at least once a week.

The occasional alcoholic drink does not negatively affect your health – in fact, some studies show that drinking up to 1 or 2 glasses of red wine 3 to 4 times a week can actually *benefit* your health.

However, alcohol abuse such as **alcoholism** (dependence on alcohol) or **binge-drinking** (drinking more than half the recommended weekly intake in one session) are both seriously damaging to one's health: they can cause liver damage, brain damage, numerous forms of cancer and death.

Units

Doctors recommend that the weekly limit of alcohol intake is no more than...

- 14 units per week for <u>women</u>
- 21 units per week for <u>men</u>

What is a unit?

One pint of strong lager (5-6% alcohol)   = 3 units
One pint of normal strength cider (5-6% alcohol)   = 3 units
One large glass of normal wine (13% alcohol)   = 2½ units
One pint of normal strength lager (3-4% alcohol)   = 2 units
One small glass of normal wine (13% alcohol)   = 2 units
One bottle of normal alcopops (5% alcohol)   = 1½ units
One small (25ml) shot of spirits (40% alcohol)   = 1 unit

DRUGS

There are three main types of illegal drug:

Stimulants	Drugs which give you energy and make you feel wide awake	*e.g. amphetamines (speed), cocaine, crack, and ecstasy*
Depressants	Drugs which dull your senses and make you feel very calm and relaxed	*e.g. cannabis and heroin*
Hallucinogens	Drugs which make you see or hear things that aren't there	*e.g. LSD and "magic" mushrooms*

Be careful!
Depressants do <u>not</u> make you depressed!

All illegal drugs are dangerous, and many are potentially addictive. Some powdered drugs (heroin, cocaine, speed) are often 'cut' with other substances like talc or washing powder, which are dangerous if inhaled, swallowed or injected. Many drugs will give the user a very unpleasant and lengthy 'come-down' after the initial, pleasurable effects have worn off.

Illegal drugs are grouped into three categories, depending on the danger they pose to the drug user (and those around them). Dealing or possessing large quantities of any illegal drug is a very serious offence, and can result in a lengthy prison sentence.

Class A:	Extremely dangerous drugs	*Ecstasy, LSD, heroin, cocaine, crack, magic mushrooms*
Class B:	Very dangerous drugs	*Amphetamines (speed), methylphenidate (ritalin), pholcodine*
Class C:	Dangerous drugs	*Cannabis, tranquilisers, some painkillers, gamma hydroxybutyrate (GHB), ketamine*

EFFECTS ON DEVELOPMENT

Smoking, alcohol and illegal drugs not only affect a person's physical health; they can also have a significant effect on intellectual, social and emotional wellbeing. Small amounts of alcohol may be beneficial, but experts say that *no amount* of smoking or illegal drugs are beneficial (though some people do use cannabis as a painkiller for conditions like Multiple Sclerosis).

	Effects on development		
Addiction	Physical	Intellectual	Social / emotional
Cigarettes	Cancer, organ failure, heart attack, heart disease	Short-term de-stressing effect	May be seen as an antisocial habit and avoided by non-smokers
Alcohol	Cirrhosis of the liver, liver failure, dizziness, convulsions	Impaired concentration, brain damage, drunkenness	Social isolation, depression, inability to work, may turn to crime to fund habit
Drugs	Damage to veins / nose, HIV, heart attack, coma, fatal overdose, stroke, convulsions	Paranoia, confusion, memory loss, flashbacks, poor concentration	Depression, social isolation, inability to work, lethargy, self-hatred, may turn to crime to fund habit

Addictions to anything are *very* dangerous to one's health, and can cause sudden or prolonged, painful deaths.

ENVIRONMENTAL INFLUENCES

Environmental influences are things that sometimes we have little control over. Environmental influences on health cover the following areas:

- Pollution
- Noise
- Access to health care
- Food quality and availability
- House type and location
- Education

POLLUTION

Air pollution

During the industrial revolution of the 18th and 19th centuries, air pollution became a major problem, as factories churned out waste products such as carbon monoxide. Now the major air pollutant in the UK is from vehicle exhaust fumes.

Global warming (or the 'greenhouse effect') refers to an increase in the average temperature of the earth; this is a form of air pollution, as it results largely from CO_2 (carbon dioxide) emissions caused by humans. Added to this is the problem of the thinning ozone layer (part of the earth's atmosphere), caused mainly by the release of CFC's into the atmosphere. This causes increased risk of sunburn and skin cancer.

Air pollution can cause asthma, bronchitis, lung cancer and other respiratory problems. It can make cities unpleasant for children to play out in, and it can cause stress and anxiety for those who suffer it regularly.

Water pollution

Because humans are at the top of the food chain, we are particularly vulnerable to water pollution; even if it doesn't contaminate our drinking water directly, if it affects the plants and animals we eat, it enters our bodies in that way.

Some causes of water pollution:

- poorly-treated or untreated human sewage
- chemicals from detergents or fertilisers
- acid pollution of lakes from acid soils
- acid rain caused by factories burning sulphur dioxide
- carbon dioxide discharges from factories
- chemical waste and industrial by-products

Water pollution can cause diarrhoea, food poisoning, dysentery, digestive disorders and even death. There will be some minimal effects on emotional wellbeing (e.g. increased fear and anxiety about drinking contaminated water), but the main danger is to physical health.

Land pollution

Humans generate a lot of waste, from food packaging, junk mail, and business and industrial waste; in the UK, this all goes to landfill sites (tips). Currently, there is not a *great* danger to human health or development from this, but space is running out, so one day there may be a problem. Much of the waste in tips could be recycled, which would lessen the impact on the environment and on human health and development.

Noise 'pollution'

Noise pollution is any unwanted man-made sound that penetrates the environment, and causes stress or annoyance to people. It is not really 'pollution', as it does not really *damage* humans or the environment, but it does detract from overall wellbeing. Some sources of noise pollution are:

- Traffic
- Machinery
- PA systems
- Concerts
- Factories
- Aircraft
- Construction work
- Alarms
- Barking dogs
- Loud music
- People shouting
- Funfairs

Noise pollution can negatively affect someone's social and emotional wellbeing, by causing stress, irritation, neighbourhood disputes and sleeplessness. This in turn can have an effect upon someone's physical and intellectual wellbeing.

ACCESS TO HEALTH SERVICES

The National Health Service (NHS) was created in 1948, to provide free healthcare for everyone regardless of income. Before that, healthcare was only open to those who could afford to pay for it. However, today there are long waiting lists and some say that standards are slipping, so many people choose to go private. People also often complain that they can't get an appointment to see their GP as quick as they would like.

Everybody pays for the NHS through their taxes, but some people who earn a high wage have enough money to pay for private care. Access to private healthcare can often be quicker than NHS waiting lists, but of course, not everybody can afford it. NHS

dentists are now very scarce, so dental care is increasingly closed off to the poorest people. Clearly, lack of access to adequate health care could negatively affect someone's physical health. This in turn could make them depressed, anxious or frustrated.

Lack of access

Sometimes there is a '**postcode lottery**': some people who fall within the boundaries of one healthcare trust may have a shorter wait and/or better treatment than someone who falls into the area of another trust, which seems incredibly unfair.

At times there is an **inverse law** with regard to health care: this is when the people most in need of health care (e.g. the poorest sectors of society) are those with the worst health care provision; this can be a fairly common occurrence in the NHS.

> ### Be careful!
> Lack of money to access healthcare may be seen as a _social_ factor: someone may have little money because their job is poorly paid. Or it could be classed as _lifestyle_: perhaps they are just lazy or they waste money. But if someone has little or no control over where they live and how much money they have, it seems to be _environmental_.

HOUSING

People in lower classes have less choice about where and how they live (so this is partly environmental, and partly social). Many people cannot afford to buy a house of their own, and have to rent a house off the local authority (a council house).

Poor housing and neighbourhoods are often associated with:

- Overcrowding (especially in bedrooms)
- Poor building maintenance, so risk of accidents
- Dirt and dampness, causing breathing problems
- Poor hygiene and cleanliness
- Antisocial behaviour
- Less or no outdoor space for children to play
- Poor local facilities (shops, leisure centres)
- Noisy neighbours and neighbour disputes
- Old, poor quality furniture

- Poor ventilation
- Higher crime rates
- Busy roads
- Poor lighting
- Litter / graffiti
- Increased pollution
- Worse local schools
- Drug problems
- Fear of other people

The effects of these on physical development is that there may be more accidents around the house or on busy roads, and children will be unable to exercise somewhere safe, which could make them overweight. People may also develop breathing difficulties from the damp, stale air inside their house, and the exhaust fumes outside.

The social development of anyone living in such an area could be drastically affected: older people or families may feel too scared to leave the house to socialise, and teenagers may suffer socially because there is nowhere for them to meet up and have fun together. This could turn them to crime, drugs and antisocial behaviour. Emotionally, many residents may feel stressed, anxious, apathetic, threatened, trapped, angry, socially isolated and helpless. Older residents in particular may feel they are only safe in large numbers – e.g. church groups – and they may not leave their house unless absolutely necessary.

EDUCATION

Generally, most people send their children to whichever schools are nearest to where they live. Living in or near a poor neighbourhood often means that the local schools are highly populated with poor children. The poorest inner-city schools can often have a lower rate of GCSE attainment, and higher rates of truancy, drugs or violence than schools in more affluent areas. This is both environmental *and* social, because it depends on where you live as well as how much money you have.

Living in a poor area and attending a poor school affects intellectual development, and can cause someone to achieve badly in their exams, so they may go on to get poorly paid jobs in the future; this causes a **circle of deprivation**. There may also be an increased risk of bullying or poor behaviour in such schools, which can be a source of stress, fear and anxiety.

Employment

Employment is obviously related to education, but also to location. It could be that one town is desperate for factory workers, while another has an abundance of them. But since it is not always possible or convenient to move house to where the jobs are, unemployment is a very real problem for some people. Others may be forced to do a job they don't enjoy, or one with a poor wage, or they may have to rely on **state benefits**. Rich people never face this problem, so this problem is both social *and* environmental.

DEFINING HEALTH

Being 'healthy' means different things to different people. Some people may consider themselves to be 'healthy' even when they have the flu; other people may think that being 'healthy' just means eating a sensible diet. To improve one's health, one must first understand what health actually *is*.

DEFINITIONS OF HEALTH

Health can be defined positively, negatively, or holistically. Each definition has its strengths and weaknesses.

Positive definition

The positive definition says that 'health' is being fit, feeling well and having normal blood pressure, weight, **Body Mass Index**, etc.

People who define health positively believe that health is maintained by exercising, eating healthily and doing things in moderation.

The positive definition is good because it focuses on what someone *does* have in their favour. And most people do agree that health is maintained by eating healthily and exercising. However, according to this definition, someone may be fit and 'healthy' but have a terminal illness.

Negative definition

The negative definition states that 'health' is <u>not</u> being ill, diseased, unfit, run down or unable to function normally.

Health professionals often tend to use the negative definition: they call it the **"biomedical model"**: they believe that health is being free from disease or illness, and health problems arise when abnormal things occur physically in the body.

The negative definition is a good one to use because it is viewed by health professionals to be the correct definition of health. However, because it focuses on *visible* problems, a patient might feel ill or claim to be in pain, but there's no evidence of illness or why they should be in pain. There may be many causes of ill health, and it is not merely limited to things that go on in the body. For example, a close friend dying might cause someone to become run down and ill, yet the trigger for this illness was an emotional problem.

Holistic definition

Whereas the positive and negative definitions of health tend to just look at the physical side of things, the holistic definition examines all aspects of a person's life (holistic means 'wholeness'.) So holistic practitioners say that being 'healthy' is having physical, mental, emotional, spiritual, social and all-round wellbeing.

The World Health Organisation defines health as "a state of complete physical, mental and social wellbeing, not merely the absence of disease or infirmity" – this is a holistic definition.

People who use the holistic definition feel that health is maintained by exercising, eating healthily, not being stressed, being mentally stable, having good relationships, relaxing and feeling at peace with yourself.

The holistic definition is useful because it considers every aspect of a person's life, not just the physical things. This is good because generally speaking, if someone has a condition such as schizophrenia, we probably wouldn't say they are 'healthy'. However, it may be too broad a definition, and it could overlook the details of a person's health. Also, most people do not believe that you need to (e.g.) have happy relationships with others in order to be 'healthy'.

FITNESS

Fitness, like health, can be defined or measured in various ways. For example:

- Speed
- **Stamina**
- **Agility**

- Strength
- Heart rate
- Power

- Flexibility
- Muscle tone
- Lung capacity

- Frequency of exercise
- Blood pressure
- **Body mass index**

Health and fitness needn't go together: someone could be fit but unhealthy (e.g. an athlete with flu), or healthy but unfit (e.g. an older person who uses a zimmer frame, but who doesn't have an illness at the moment).

Someone may not possess all the above 'types' of fitness: e.g. they may be unable to touch their toes, but they can run a marathon; or they might be able to lift 20 stone in weights, but be unable to run 500 metres. Sometimes, people might be fat on one part of their body, but be skinny elsewhere.

HEALTH PROMOTION

Health promotion is important to many people: a nation of healthy people is more happy and productive: everyone benefits from this.

WHO PROMOTES HEALTH

Many people wish to promote good health, for example:

- Governments
- Patients
- Health workers
- International bodies

- Schools
- Doctors
- Support groups
- Employers

- Celebrities
- Businesses
- Pressure groups
- Bereaved families

AIMS

Some aims of health promotion are:

- To improve levels of fitness through exercise
- To immunise people against preventable diseases
- To make people understand the causes of illnesses
- To prevent alcoholism and binge drinking
- To prevent disease and ill health generally
- To promote safe sex and prevent the spread of sexually transmitted diseases and unwanted pregnancies
- To inform people about medical advances and available treatments
- To stop people drinking and driving
- To discourage people from taking illegal drugs, and help those who are addicted to them to give up
- To help and encourage people to give up smoking
- To encourage people to eat more healthily (e.g. five portions of fruit and vegetables per day)
- To better treat existing health problems that people may have

APPROACHES

Health promotion can be approached in three ways:

★ The biomedical approach

★ The societal change approach

★ The educational / behaviour approach

BIOMEDICAL APPROACH

The biomedical approach takes medical action to improve people's health. This is carried out by doctors or other medical practitioners and experts, and is usually done with the full consent of the patient. A biomedical campaign may be supported by a law (e.g. a law saying all sexually active women must be offered a cervical smear test every three years).

Some examples of biomedical health interventions are:
- Immunisations
- Check-ups
- Smear tests
- Breast screening
- Tablets and drugs
- Health visitors
- Well women / men clinics
- Free contraceptives
- Operations

Advantages of a biomedical approach

☺ Medical action can prevent many health problems, and prevention is better than cure

☺ The tests and medications work on the majority of people

☺ Biomedical campaigns can reach nearly everyone (e.g. every woman of a certain age who is registered with a GP will be invited for breast cancer screening)

☺ Many people will happily have tests and medicines which help them improve their health

☺ There are a wide variety of medical drugs and treatments available, so there should be something available to help most people

☺ It can help people get quick results – e.g. a stomach stapling operation works much faster than losing weight through diet and exercise

☺ Medical intervention is useful as a back-up, if (e.g. obese) people were unable or unwilling to change their behaviour as a result of an educational campaign

☺ The public generally have faith in science and medicine, so will probably believe it if they're told they need treatment

Disadvantages of a biomedical approach

☹ Some people are afraid of medical treatment (e.g. the MMR jab)

☹ People might not understand *why* they need it

☹ It might be hard for people to get to the clinic

☹ It may treat the problem, but not the root cause (e.g. fattening up a person with anorexia)

☹ It may just give a 'quick fix', the effects of which don't last

☹ Some people may ignore the strategies offered (e.g. smear tests)

☹ Some intervention strategies are quite drastic and unpleasant (e.g. forcing someone to come off heroin and to 'go cold turkey')

☹ People simply might not know about the treatments that are on offer

SOCIETAL CHANGE APPROACH

This method of improving health affects all individuals in society, through laws, restrictions and policies. For example:

- Raising the age of consent
- Anti-smoking laws
- Legalising / criminalising drugs
- Banning cigarette adverts
- Targets for doctors to meet
- Compulsory healthy school dinners
- Longer sentences for drug dealers
- Prosecuting parents of obese children

Only the government can change the laws in the UK, but since they are not health professionals, they will need to acquire their information from somewhere. The laws they introduce (or get rid of) may be based on research by a particular person or company (e.g. into the effects of smoking on children's health) or as a result of public opinion (e.g. if everyone thinks the age of consent should be 18). They will also need to have close links with the police and the legal system, to decide how any law-breakers should be dealt with.

Advantages of a societal change approach

- ☺ It's hard to miss changes in the law as they are usually well-publicised
- ☺ The strategies can be enforced by law, unlike biomedical or educational campaigns
- ☺ People may listen if it becomes law, and realise it's serious (e.g. people tend to think illegal drugs are dangerous, from the simple fact that they're illegal)
- ☺ People may be scared of the punishments that come from breaking the law, so abide by it
- ☺ If something is illegal, it may also be seen as morally wrong

Disadvantages of a societal change approach

- ☹ People might rebel and think it's cool to break the law
- ☹ It often takes several years for laws to take full effect
- ☹ It might be difficult to enforce laws (e.g. raising the age of consent to 18)
- ☹ There are currently many laws which are broken (e.g. many people under 18 who buy and drink alcohol) so maybe laws don't work
- ☹ Banning something (e.g. illegal drugs) just pushes it into the back streets rather than stopping it altogether
- ☹ If something is illegal then it's unregulated: criminal drug dealers may 'cut' drugs with other substances and make them even more dangerous
- ☹ People might group together to protest or rebel
- ☹ Introducing a new law (e.g. against cigarettes for 16-18 years olds) doesn't help tackle people who are already addicted to something
- ☹ People may view some laws as too dictatorial and harsh

EDUCATIONAL / BEHAVIOUR APPROACH

This approach explains things to people (e.g. symptoms of an illness, or the risks of binge drinking,) to help them understand things more fully. The idea is that this in turn should change people's behaviour.

Some examples of educational and behavioural campaigns are:

- School talks
- Rehabilitation centres
- Support groups
- Documentaries
- Books
- Letters through the post
- Leaflets
- Care worker visits
- TV adverts
- Websites
- Magazines
- Billboards
- Demonstrations
- Posters
- Phone lines (e.g. NHS Direct)
- Pressure group campaigns

Educational approach focuses

The educational / behavioural approach always works by giving people knowledge in the hope that they will take action to improve their own or others' health. The details given to people can have three main focuses:

Information focus:	Increases awareness of health issues simply by giving information to people, e.g. about the effects of cigarettes, which foods are unhealthy, how much exercise per week is recommended by experts
Activity focus:	Provides people with methods they can use to improve their health, e.g. ways to incorporate exercise into your day, strategies to give up smoking or cut down on alcohol
Medical focus:	Makes people aware of medical practices and procedures that can treat or help prevent ill health, e.g. telling people about immunisation, breast cancer screening, or smear tests. A biomedical campaign will often be coupled with an educational campaign with a medical focus, in order to let people know about the biomedical strategies available.

Be careful!

A campaign which gives people (e.g.) immunisations or tablets is a biomedical campaign. But a campaign which just tells people they should be immunised or take some tablets is an educational / behavioural campaign!

Advantages of an educational/ behavioural approach

☺ It gives people information and allows them to make an informed decision for themselves, rather than forcing them into something

☺ It can be targeted at a specific group of people – e.g. warnings about anorexia could be put into teenage girls' magazines

☺ "**Pester power**" works quite well, so children could (e.g.) keep asking their parents to buy them a bike so they can exercise

☺ It's good for people to understand more about illnesses

☺ If enough people are educated, it becomes 'common sense'

☺ People may not have actually known (e.g. that fatty foods are bad for you) and so once they know, they may decide to change their behaviour

☺ There are lots of strategies for helping someone change their behaviour (see previous page), that can be tailored to the individual

☺ Lots of people do watch television, read magazines, use the internet (etc.) so campaigns can reach a lot of people

Disadvantages of an educational/ behavioural approach

☹ A television campaign might not reach people who play video games, read books, go out, watch unusual channels, or who don't watch much television at all

☹ Very young children will be too young to understand the campaign

☹ People might feel they're being preached or dictated to, so resist being told what to do and rebel even more

☹ People change channels, make coffee, use the toilet (etc.) during advert breaks, so may easily miss an advert

☹ People may already be educated about health issues, but just not care

☹ Health warnings (e.g. on fatty foods or alcohol) may not work, as the ones on cigarettes haven't stopped people smoking

☹ Billboards and posters are often ignored or not even noticed

☹ Documentaries are often not watched by the people who most need to watch them

☹ People are unlikely to search for or locate a health website, and are unlikely to discover it by chance

☹ Websites or emails are only available to people who have internet access

☹ People might not want to listen or change

☹ A leaflet can be thrown away without being looked at

☹ People may still be in denial about their safety: e.g. many people believe that they won't get lung cancer, even though they smoke heavily

☹ School talks don't reach children who truant

☹ People might feel that the benefits of something (e.g. the fun of binge drinking) outweigh any drawbacks (possible liver failure in later life)

COMBINING APPROACHES

Many health promotion campaigns use several methods at once:

Campaign:	To prevent skin cancer
Biomedical:	Free check-ups for the public to go to if they're worried
Educational:	A TV advert warning of the risk of skin cancer
Societal change:	A policy which says all suntan lotion must be Factor 15 or higher

Campaign:	To cut obesity rates in children and teenagers
Biomedical:	Walk-in health clinics for obese children / teens
Educational:	A website set up for children and teens to share ideas and tips for losing weight
Societal change:	A law banning unhealthy foods from being eaten in schools

Campaign:	To reduce lung cancer caused by smoking
Biomedical:	Free nicotine patches and chewing gum
Educational:	Talks by school nurses explaining how to give up smoking
Societal change:	A law making smoking in public places illegal

Generally speaking, one campaign – whether biomedical, educational / behavioural, or societal change – is not going to have *enormous* impacts on everyone in the country. Combining approaches from different areas can increase the likelihood of there being an improvement, but the success rate of a campaign is never going to be 100%.

Sample Examination Papers

This section contains three Sample Examination Papers for you to try. Before you attempt one of these, you should use the Fast Facts section to ensure that you fully understand all the information presented there.

When you do one of these papers, you should give yourself 1½ hours under exam conditions, and complete as many answers as fully as you can. Then mark your paper using the Mark Scheme.

SAMPLE EXAMINATION #1

1

Adam is 6, and his brother, Sam is three years old: they live with their mother, Shannon. They are both growing and developing normally for their age. Adam enjoys football and he plays it in an after-school club once a week. The children's father lived with Shannon until two years ago; he has now moved abroad and has a new wife.

(a) Explain the difference between growth and development. **(4)**

(b) Identify **two** factors that could affect Adam's physical development. **(2)**

(c) Discuss how Adam's development might be affected by playing football. **(8)**

(d) Sam is meeting the norms expected of a boy his age. Explain what is meant by 'norms'. **(4)**

(e) Explain how a child's intellectual development will progress during infancy. **(4)**

(f) Discuss how Adam and Sam's development could be affected by not having a father in their lives. **(8)**

(Total 30 marks)

2   Gerald is 59 and is about to retire from his job as the Managing Director of a haulage company. Gerald's wife divorced him four years ago, after she discovered that she was homosexual; she now lives with her female partner. Gerald tries to eat sensibly, and he has recently started going swimming again, which he is good at and enjoys.

(a) What life stage is Gerald in?   **(1)**

(b) Gerald is fully mature. Explain what 'maturation' is.   **(3)**

(c) Identify **three** effects of ageing that Gerald may be noticing in himself.   **(3)**

(d) Gerald describes himself as middle class. Discuss how belonging to the middle classes can affect someone's physical, intellectual, social and emotional development.   **(8)**

(e) Explain **three** ways in which swimming could positively affect Gerald's physical development.   **(10)**

(f) Gerald has five grandchildren whom he sees every weekend, and they have all been socialised since a young age. Explain the importance of early socialisation in children.   **(5)**

(Total 30 marks)

3   Governments, charities and other organisations often run health promotion campaigns. The following information was published by the charity Cancer Research UK.

> **Lung Cancer and Smoking Statistics**
>
> Tobacco consumption is recognised as the UK's single greatest cause of preventable illness and early death, with more than 120,000 people dying each year from smoking-related diseases. Around 90% of lung cancer cases in the UK are caused by tobacco smoking. In Britain the highest rates of smoking are in the 20-24 age-group, with 37% of men and 38% of women this age recorded as smokers. The number of people who smoke regularly has been declining steadily since the 1950s, but there are still around 13 million adult cigarette smokers in Great Britain. A further 2 million adults smoke pipes and/or cigars.

Source: Cancer Research UK, 2004

(a)   From the information given, identify **one** piece of evidence which suggests that smoking is a significant problem in the UK.   **(1)**

(b)   Health can be defined in a number of different ways. Three ways are holistically, positively, and negatively. Explain what is meant by the holistic definition of health.   **(3)**

(c)   Health promotion campaigns can be approached in different ways, including:
- the biomedical approach
- the educational / behaviour approach
- the societal change approach

(i)   Explain **four** potential barriers to the success of an educational / behavioural health promotion campaign.   **(8)**

(ii)   Discuss the possible success of an anti-smoking campaign which uses a societal change approach.   **(10)**

(d)   Describe **one** negative effect on each area of development caused by smoking:

- Physical
- Intellectual
- Emotional
- Social   **(8)**

(Total 30 marks)

TOTAL FOR PAPER: 90 marks

▶ *The Mark Scheme for this paper is on page 86*

SAMPLE EXAMINATION #2

1

Georgia is 14 years old and she is keen on horse riding. Her parents own a horse, which Georgia helps to look after. She goes to see her horse after school, to clean out the stables and exercise it. At the weekends, she goes on longer rides, often with a local horse-riding club for teenagers.

(a) Georgia is going through puberty. Explain what puberty is. **(2)**

(b) Identify **three** physical changes that will happen to Georgia during puberty which will **not** happen to a boy. **(3)**

(c) Discuss the impact of peer pressure upon teenagers' social and emotional development. **(8)**

(d) Discuss the possible effects of being involved in horse riding and caring for a horse on Georgia's physical, intellectual, social and emotional development. **(8)**

(e) Georgia has developed many gross and fine motor skills. Explain the difference between gross and fine motor skills **(4)**

(f) Georgia is in the life stage of Adolescence. Identify the other five main life stages in chronological order. **(5)**

(Total 30 marks)

2   Thomas is 17 years old and has Down's Syndrome. He attends college three days a week and is trying to become more independent. He currently lives with his mum and dad, but hopes that he will be able to move out of home soon and ideally to get a job.

(a) Down's Syndrome is a chromosome condition. What is a chromosome?   **(2)**

(b) Sex is determined by chromosomes. Sex chromosomes can either be XX or XY. Which will Thomas have?   **(1)**

(c) Both of Thomas's parents have blue eyes. The gene for brown eyes is dominant, and the gene for blue eyes is recessive. What was the chance of Thomas having blue eyes, and why?   **(3)**

(d) Thomas and his parents live on a very busy main road, where they experience a lot of air and noise pollution. Explain **three** ways this could have a negative effect on Thomas's development.   **(6)**

(e) Thomas has never attended a mainstream school. Discuss the impact this could have on his development.   **(10)**

(f) Thomas's friend, Anton, describes his race as Afro-Caribbean. Discuss the effects on a person's social and emotional development of being an Afro-Caribbean person living in Britain today.   **(8)**

(Total 30 marks)

3   **Childhood obesity rates per hundred in England in 2004**

		Age in years		
		2 - 10	**11- 15**	**All under 16**
Boys	Overweight	15	13	14
	Obese	16	24	19
	Total overweight & obese	**31**	**37**	**33**
Girls	Overweight	15	19	17
	Obese	13	27	19
	Total overweight & obese	**28**	**46**	**35**

Source: Department of Health (2005) Health Survey for England 2004

(a) From the information given;

(i)   Identify **one** trend which is occurring.   **(1)**

(ii) Identify and explain **three** possible reasons why the trend identified
in (i) may be occurring.   **(6)**

(b) Health can be promoted in different ways:
- the biomedical approach
- the educational / behaviour approach
- the societal change approach

(i)   Explain which approach is being used if a campaign to treat the
effects of obesity focuses on giving slimming tablets to children who
are obese.   **(3)**

(ii) Explain which approach is being used if an obesity-prevention
campaign focuses on having adverts on television informing
children that they should eat at least five portions of fruit and
vegetables per day.   **(3)**

(iii) Evaluate the possible success of the campaigns identified in (i) and (ii) to reduce levels of obesity among children and adolescents aged 2 to 15. **(8)**

(c) Discuss the possible effects of obesity on an adolescent's emotional and social development. **(9)**

(Total 30 marks)

TOTAL FOR PAPER: 90 MARKS

► *The Mark Scheme for this paper is on page 92*

SAMPLE EXAMINATION #3

1

Louise is 36 and she is married to David, who is 39. They have a two sons: Harry, who is 7 years old, and James, who is 3 years old. Harry has severe epilepsy and requires round-the-clock care. Louise has given up work and is staying at home to look after her sons.

(a) (i) What life stage is James in?   **(1)**

    (ii) Name **three** gross motor skills that most children will have acquired by the time they are 3 years old.   **(3)**

(b) When James was born, he possessed all the innate reflexes which are expected of a newborn baby. Identify and explain **four** innate reflexes.   **(8)**

(c) James can use telegraphic speech. Explain what is meant by the term 'telegraphic speech', and give an example   **(2)**

(d) Harry and James have formed a strong attachment to their mother. Explain the importance of a child forming an attachment to a parent or carer during infancy.   **(6)**

(e) Discuss the effects of having a son with severe epilepsy upon David and Louise's social and emotional development.   **(10)**

(Total 30 marks)

2   Annabel is 26 years old, and a single mother to three children, aged six, four and two years old. Sometimes, Annabel is so busy that she doesn't have time to cook. She often goes to the chip shop, or grazes on crisps throughout the day. Annabel is obese and does not like exercise. She works in a cosmetics warehouse as a packer – this involves collecting goods from around the warehouse and arranging them into a box. She works 24 hours per week, and earns the minimum wage; Annabel also receives Income Support. She and her children live in a house with two bedrooms, provided by the council. Annabel feels stressed from her hectic lifestyle, and so she smokes cannabis most nights to help her relax.

(a)   Annabel has been told by a health worker that she is not living a healthy lifestyle. Explain what is meant by the term 'lifestyle'.   **(2)**

(b)   Discuss whether smoking cannabis is a beneficial way for Annabel to cope with the demands of her lifestyle.   **(6)**

(c)   Identify and explain **three** ways that Annabel's lifestyle could be improved.   **(10)**

(d)   Annabel and her two older children are all overweight. Annabel claims that her weight is due to her genes, and that her children are also overweight because they have inherited her genes.

Discuss how an understanding of nature and nurture could help Annabel improve her health and well-being.   **(12)**

(Total 30 marks)

3   Governments, charities and other organisations often conduct research into health issues and illnesses. The following information was published by the Alzheimer's Society.

<u>Incidence of Alzheimer's Disease and Dementia</u>

Dementia currently affects over 750,000 people in the UK. Dementia affects one person in 20 aged over 65 years and one person in five over 80 years of age. It is estimated that by 2010 there will be about 870,000 people with dementia in the UK. This is expected to rise to over 1.8 million people with dementia by 2050.

Source: Alzheimer's Society, 2004

(a) From the information given:

    (i) Identify **one** trend which is predicted.   **(1)**

    (ii) Explain **one** social factor which could be a cause of Alzheimer's disease and dementia.   **(2)**

    (iii) Explain **one** genetic factor which could be a cause of Alzheimer's disease and dementia.   **(2)**

(b) Explain **two** factors that may affect society's attitude towards dementia and Alzheimer's disease.   **(4)**

(c) Health and well-being can be defined in different ways. Explain what is meant by the positive definition of health.   **(3)**

(d) One aim of health promotion is to prevent people from taking illegal drugs. Explain **five** other possible aims of health promotion.   **(10)**

(e) Explain **four** negative long-term effects on a person's physical, intellectual, social and emotional development of having an addiction to illegal drugs.   **(8)**

(Total 30 marks)

TOTAL FOR PAPER: 90 MARKS

▶ *The Mark Scheme for this paper is on page 99*

Mark Schemes

This section contains the Mark Schemes for the Sample Examination Papers. These Mark Schemes should be used as a guide only, and do not constitute model answers. For model answers, see pages 107 to 131.

For some questions – especially the longer 'Discuss...' questions – there are a range of responses a candidate could give in order to achieve full marks. Such questions are shown with an asterisk[*]. Use judgement to decide whether your answer is sufficiently accurate: you may need to consult the Fast Facts section, or to ask a parent, teacher or friend.

MARK SCHEME #1

Question		Expected answers	Marks	
			Distribution	Total
1	(a)	*Growth*: a physical increase in size and weight *Development*: an increase in skills or abilities. 　　Can be physical, intellectual, social or 　　emotional abilities	(4 marks) for a full explanation	(4)
	(b)*	Identification of any **two** of the following: 　• 　Exercise　　• 　Family 　• 　Diet　　　　• 　Parents 　• 　Encouragement　• 　Self-concept 　• 　Health　　　• 　School	(1 mark) x (2 points identified)	(2)
	(c) *	For full marks, candidates must identify one positive and one negative point for each area of development: Physical: 　• 　*Positive* – encourage muscle 　　development, or he may improve his 　　cardiovascular system 　• 　*Negative* – it could tire him out, he may 　　get seriously injured Intellectual: 　• 　*Positive* – he has to learn the complex 　　rules 　• 　*Negative* – he may have less time for 　　school work, or abandon school in favour 　　of football when he is older Social: 　• 　*Positive* – he could make lots of friends, 　　or be a good sport / good loser 　• 　*Negative* – he may get bullied if he does 　　badly, or he may struggle to get on with 　　the other players Emotional: 　• 　*Positive* – he could have fun, and 　　develop a confidence and self-esteem 　• 　*Negative* – it may lower his self-esteem 　　if he does badly, or he may feel jealous 　　of other players who are better than him	(1 mark) x (8 points identified)	(8)

(d)	*Norm*: an average milestone that a person is expected to reach at a given age. A relevant example should be given for the full 4 marks. E.g. a child should say their first words at approximately 12 months of age	(3 marks) for full explanation (1 mark) for example	(4)
(e) *	For full marks, candidates should explain at least **two** areas of intellectual development during infancy, including any of the following: • Learn up to around 200 words • Use telegraphic speech • Know names of people, objects, animals • Learn through playing with toys • Learn through modelling / copying adults	(2 marks) x (2 points explained)	(4)
(f) *	For full marks, candidates must identify **one** positive and **one** negative point for each area of development: Physical: • *Positive* – may have to do more around the house, (e.g. housework, DIY) and so get really good at it • *Negative* – may miss out on football coaching and physical games Intellectual: • *Positive* – may learn to be more independent / responsible • *Negative* – may struggle with school work if their mother doesn't have enough time to help them Social: • *Positive* – may feel socially confident if they take over the father's role as 'man of the house', or may fit in well with other children with absent fathers • *Negative* – may not understand gender roles or familial relationships Emotional: • *Positive* – may become much closer to their mother and develop a stronger bond • *Negative* – may feel upset or abandoned by their father	(1 mark) x (8 points made)	(8)
	Total marks for Question 1		**(30)**

Question		Expected answers	Marks	
			Distribution	Total
2	(a)	Middle adulthood	(1 mark)	(1)
	(b)	*Maturation:* A natural 'body clock', genetically programmed since birth. It triggers the onset of physical changes such as puberty, balding and the menopause. It is independent of environment or lifestyle, and is found consistently in people all over the world.	(3 marks) for a full answer	(3)
	(c) *	Any **three** of the following: • Grey hair • More illnesses • Wrinkles • Stiff joints • Balding • Aches and pains • Loss of strength, stamina or muscle tone	(1 mark) x (3 points made)	(3)
	(d)*	For full marks, candidates must identify **one** positive and **one** negative point for each area of development, including any of the following: Physical: • *Positive* – they could have more money to spend on leisure activities – e.g. horse riding, which will improve their fitness • *Negative* – they may have less free time to pursue leisure activities; they may be busy, so just eat fast food on the run Intellectual: • *Positive* – they may have a more intellectually challenging job, which keeps the mind active • *Negative* – there may be more stress from a difficult job Social: • *Positive* – they may have more free time to go out socialising with friends and family • *Negative* – there may be pressure to take 'designer drugs' such as cocaine, or to attend certain events to keep in with cliques Emotional: • *Positive* – they may be happier due to being able to afford a nicer house and	(1 mark) x (8 points made)	(8)

Question		Expected answers	Marks Distribution	Total
		possessions, they may live in a low-crime area • *Negative* – they may get into serious debt if they lose their job and still have high monthly outgoings		
	(e)*	Explanations of **three** improvements, including any of the following: • *Cardiovascular system:* it will improve his heart and lungs to do cardiovascular exercise regularly • *Muscle tone / wastage:* it will increase Gerald's muscle mass or prevent wastage of muscles • *Speed / stamina:* Gerald will be able to exercise for longer periods of time • *Joints:* it will loosen up his joints or prevent them from becoming stiff	(3-4 marks) x (3 effects explained fully)	(10)
	(f)	Early socialisation allows children to form attachments to a range of people, enabling them to make more successful attachments in future. They also learn norms, values and their culture.	(5 marks) for full explanation	(5)
		Total marks for Question 2		**(30)**

Question		Expected answers	Marks	
			Distribution	Total
3	(a)	Any **one** of the following: • It's the single greatest cause of preventable illness and early death • More than 120,000 people die from smoking related diseases each year • 90% of lung cancer caused by smoking • 37 / 38% of men / women are smokers • 13+2 million adult smokers in Britain	(1 mark) x (1 point)	(1)
	(b)	*Holistic definition:* not just the absence of illness or disease, but all the aspects of wellbeing: physical, emotional, social, intellectual, spiritual, health, fitness, diet, etc.	(3 marks) for full explanation	(3)
	(c) (i) *	For full marks, **four** barriers must be explained, including any of the following: • A television advert may not be seen by	(2 marks) x (4 explanations	(8)

		certain groups of people who don't watch TV, or watch other channels • People flick channels, make coffee (etc.) during television adverts • Television documentaries are not watched by many people • A leaflet can be thrown away without the recipient reading it • Billboard adverts are often not noticed, or only noticed by motorists • School talks will not reach children who truant • Teens hate school talks and often just ignore them • Warnings on food (etc.) may not work, as cigarette warnings have not worked • Websites are unlikely to be searched for or found accidentally unless someone is looking for it • Websites or emails are only used by people who have internet access • People may already be educated about the health issues, but just not care		
	(c) (ii)*	For full marks, candidates must identify a range of positive and negative points, including any of the following: *Positive* – • People may be scared of breaking the law, and so not smoke if it is illegal • If it's illegal (e.g.) to smoke, it could also be seen as morally wrong or antisocial, which adds to the pressure to give up • It could prevent people becoming addicted in the first place • People are likely to cut down or give up smoking if it's not allowed in public *Negative* – • Teenagers may ignore (e.g.) a new law which says you must be over 18 to buy cigarettes (many under 16s currently buy cigarettes even though it's illegal) • Shops may choose to ignore the laws and still sell cigarettes to under 18s	(1 mark) x (10 points explained)	(10)

		<ul><li>People may rebel against a law (e.g.) which says you can't smoke in public places, as they feel it's too draconian</li><li>More people may just smoke in secret</li><li>It can't tackle people who are already addicted</li><li>It should be done in conjunction (e.q.) with a biomedical campaign giving free nicotine patches and help giving up</li></ul>		
(d) *		For full marks, candidates must identify **one** negative effect for each area of development, including any of the following: Physical: <table><tr><td>• Lung cancer</td><td>• Mouth cancer</td></tr><tr><td>• Throat cancer</td><td>• Stomach cancer</td></tr><tr><td>• Emphysema</td><td>• Asthma</td></tr><tr><td>• Heart attacks</td><td>• Bronchitis</td></tr><tr><td>• Heart disease</td><td>• Cardiovascular</td></tr><tr><td>• Strokes</td><td> disease</td></tr></table>Intellectual: <ul><li>Smokers may find it harder to concentrate when they're having nicotine withdrawal symptoms</li></ul>Emotional: <ul><li>People may feel angry, guilty or frustrated with themselves for not being able to give up smoking</li><li>People can feel nervous or agitated with withdrawal symptoms</li></ul>Social: <ul><li>People may lose friends who don't like them smoking</li><li>When smoking becomes illegal in pubs, people may lose out on their social life</li></ul>	(2 marks) x (4 effects described)	(8)
		Total marks for Question 3		**(30)**
		TOTAL MARKS FOR EXAMINATION PAPER		**(90)**

MARK SCHEME #2

Question		Expected answers	Marks	
			Distribution	Total
1	(a)	*Puberty*: the time when secondary sexual characteristics develop and the body becomes capable of producing children.	(2 marks) for full answer	(2)
	(b)	Any **three** of the following: • hips widen • ovulation starts • vagina / womb / clitoris enlarge • menstruation begins • breasts develop	(1 mark) x (3 points)	(3)
	(c) *	For full marks, candidates must identify a range of positive and negative points, including any of the following: *Positive –* • Peers may encourage each other to be kind, generous and helpful • People can feel happy and confident that they don't succumb to peer pressure • Someone can gain friends by doing what they are encouraged to do by their peers • Someone can feel very happy to have lots of friends • It can increase a person's self-confidence if they have things in common with their friends and do the same things as them *Negative –* • Peers may encourage each other to play truant from school, or to rebel and not study hard • People may feel forced into doing illegal activities such as shoplifting or engaging in anti-social behaviour • Someone may lose friends if they refuse to do what they're being encouraged to do • Someone could be very upset if they	(1 mark) x (8 points made)	(8)

		lose friends • People may feel that they have no control over the things they do • Someone might feel guilty and upset about doing things which they know are wrong		
	(d)*	For full marks, candidates must identify **one** positive and **one** negative point for each area of development, including any of the following: Physical: • *Positive* – Georgia could get fitter by engaging in all the exercise; she will control her weight and not become fat • *Negative* – she may become tired or sustain a serious injury Intellectual: • *Positive* – she will learn a lot about horses, how to ride them and care for them • *Negative* – she may be so busy with the horses that she neglects school work Social: • *Positive* – she could make friends at the horse riding club, and attend social events • *Negative* – she may lose touch with old friends who are not interested in horses, or because she is always so busy Emotional: • *Positive* – she could feel happy that she is doing something she enjoys • *Negative* – she could feel burdened by all the responsibility she has for looking after the horse; she'll be upset when it dies	(1 mark) x (8 points made)	(8)
	(e)	*Gross motor skills*: physical skills using the large muscles of the body, such as the arms, legs, neck and torso. All locomotive skills (walking, running) are gross motor skills. *Fine motor skills*: physical skills using the small muscles of the hands and wrists to manipulate objects. For example, typing, using cutlery, drawing and writing.	(4 marks) for full explanation	(4)

(f)	• Infancy • Childhood *(Adolescence)* • Early adulthood • Middle adulthood • Later adulthood / old age	(1 mark) x (5 life stages in correct order)	(5)
	Total marks for Question 1		**(30)**

Question		Expected answers	Marks	
			Distribution	Total
2	(a)	*Chromosome:* a DNA strand coiled up into an X-shape: the carrier of hereditary characteristics, found in the nucleus of every cell.	(2 marks) for a full answer	(2)
	(b)	XY because he is male	(1 mark)	(1)
	(c)	The gene for blue eyes is recessive: this means that someone will only have blue eyes if they have two 'blue' genes. This must be the case with Thomas's parents. Therefore they can only pass on 'blue' genes to Thomas. So he will definitely have blue eyes (a 100% chance).	(1 mark) for identification + (2 marks) for full explanation	(3)
	(d) *	For full marks, candidates must fully explain **three** negative effects on development, including any of the following: *Breathing problems* – the air pollution affects physical development because he may develop lung diseases such as asthma, bronchitis or emphysema. This is because breathing unclean air regularly over a long period of time is damaging to the alveoli in the lungs. *Sleep deprivation* – the noise pollution affects all forms of development (P.I.E.S.) because he will be irritable and unable to concentrate in school; he'll feel sleepy and not at his best because he can't sleep properly *Weight* – the noise and air pollution could cause him to be overweight, because he doesn't want to exercise, because he's always tired from sleep deprivation, and outside the air is not clean. This lack of	(2 marks) x (3 points explained)	(6)

		exercise could cause him to become obese.		
	(e) *	For full marks, candidates must identify at least **one** positive and **one** negative point for each area of development, including any of the following: Physical: • *Positive* – he could develop his physical skills more easily with specialist (rather than mainstream) help from carers • *Negative* – being with other children more physically able than him could have stretched him to improve his skills more Intellectual: • *Positive* – he will be able to go at his own pace, and get an education specific to his needs from experienced staff • *Negative* – he may not realise if he is working at a far lower level than people in mainstream schools are Social: • *Positive* – he could make friends with people like himself who will understand his problems; he won't discriminate against others • *Negative* – it may come as a shock to him to go out into the 'real world' and he might not be able to cope if he gets bullied for being different Emotional: • *Positive* – he may have fun and feel confident in his achievements • *Negative* – he may feel upset, and that he has been segregated from others simply for being different	(1 mark) x (10 points made)	(10)
	(f) *	For full marks, candidates must identify a range of positive and negative points, including any of the following: *Positive* – • Most people are not at all racist, so they'll be treated just the same as a white person	(1 mark) x (8 points made)	(8)

		• They may be bilingual or multilingual • They can feel like they fit into two cultures (e.g. Jamaican culture and English culture) • They may be likely to get jobs in multicultural businesses • They may enjoy breaking any negative stereotypes associated with their race *Negative –* • They are more likely to suffer racism • They're more likely to live in poorer areas and inner cities • They are statistically less likely to do well in school • They're less likely to get a well-paid job • They are statistically more likely to be convicted of a crime • They're more likely to be the victim of crime • They are more likely to suffer social exclusion and feel lonely • People whose first language is not English may experience a language barrier		
	Total marks for Question 2			**(30)**

Question		Expected answers	Marks	
			Distribution	Total
3	(a) (i)*	Any **one** of the following: • A greater percentage of 11-15 year olds are overweight or obese than 2-10 year olds • For 11-15 year olds, girls are more likely to be overweight or obese than boys • For 2-10 year olds, boys are more likely to be overweight / obese than girls • Approximately one third of all children are overweight or obese	(1 mark) x (1 point made)	(1)
	(ii)*	For full marks, candidates must explain **three** reasons, including any of the following: • Fast food / junk food is cheaper and easier to come by than it used to be	(2 marks) x (3 points explained)	(6)

		• There are more working mothers, and people have busier lives and less time to cook healthily • Watching television and playing video games are more popular than physical games • It isn't "cool" to exercise • Children think unhealthy food tastes nicer than healthy food • People don't realise what types of food are bad for them		
	(b) (i)	A biomedical campaign, because it focuses on medical intervention to physically solve the problem. These treatments will be issued by health professionals.	(1 mark) for identification + (2 marks) for explanation	(3)
	(ii)	An educational / behavioural approach, because it focuses on giving information to people, so they can learn about the condition. This should change their behaviour accordingly.	(1 mark) for identification + (2 marks) for explanation	(3)
	(iii)*	For full marks, candidates must identify a range of positive and negative points for both campaigns, including any of the following: Biomedical: *Positive –* • The tablets could actually halt their gaining weight • It would be an option if everything else has been tried *Negative –* • It is quite drastic to give medication to children • Diet and exercise would be preferable for their overall health • It will only provide a "quick fix" and not treat the underlying cause Educational / behaviour: *Positive –* • Lots of children watch television and believe what they are told on it • It will treat one of the causes of obesity as well as the effect	(1 mark) x (8 points made)	(8)

		Negative – • Children may not see the adverts if they play video games, use the internet, or read a lot • Children may ignore / rebel against the adverts • Very young children may be too young to understand the adverts		
(c) *		For full marks, candidates should identify a range of positive and negative points, including any of the following: *Positive –* • Someone may develop a 'bubbly' personality to compensate for their weight • Someone could feel happy and comfortable with their weight and body image, and still feel attractive • They may feel pleased that they have not given in to the media images of thin women • They may take up exercise to lose weight, and have lots of fun *Negative –* • Someone may get bullied, especially at school • They may feel it is impossible for them to lose weight • They might not have any friends because they are overweight • Someone could feel upset or depressed and have a negative self-concept • They may feel ashamed of themselves for comfort eating • They may start to truant from school to escape bullies • They may give in to peer pressure (e.g. to commit crimes or take drugs) to try and make themselves more popular • They may hate themselves and self-harm or contemplate suicide	(1 mark) x (9 points made)	(9)
		Total marks for Question 3		**(30)**
		TOTAL MARKS FOR EXAMINATION PAPER		**(90)**

MARK SCHEME #3

Question		Expected answers	Marks	
			Distribution	Total
1 (a) (i)		Childhood	(1 mark)	(1)
	(ii)*	Candidates must identify **three** gross motor skills, including any of the following: • standing • kicking a ball • walking • going up stairs • running • holding head up • sitting down • crawling • jumping • climbing on sofa	(1 mark) x (3 skills identified)	(3)
	(b)	Any **four** of the following: *Moro / startle reflex* – When startled, a baby throws out his arms and legs, then pulls them back in again and grimaces *Protective reflex* – If you place a cloth over a baby's face, he will turn his head to the side, and bring his hands up to swipe away the cloth *Grasp reflex* – A baby will grasp an object placed in his hand (or sometimes foot) *Hand-to-mouth reflex* – A baby will bring an object to his mouth and begin to suck it *Rooting reflex* – If a baby's cheek is touched, he turns his head in the direction of the touch *Crawling reflex* – A baby hovered face down near a surface will show crawling movements *Walking / stepping reflex* – A baby held upright with his feet touching the ground will make stepping movements	(2 marks) x (4 reflexes explained)	(8)
	(c)	*Telegraphic speech*: two-word sentences that are grammatically correct and make sense. E.g. "Nana come" "Doggy wet" "Kick ball"	(2 marks) for explan- ation and example	(2)
	(d)	An early specific attachment to a parent is the norm; it acts as a blueprint on which the infant bases further relationships. Without a successful	(6 marks) for a full explanation	(6)

		first attachment, children are prone to being socially isolated and having few friends. They are more likely to be bullied or bully others, to struggle in school, be unemployed, have weak or destructive relationships, suffer depression, self-harm, attempt suicide and to live a dysfunctional life.		
	(e)*	For full marks, candidates should give a range of positive and negative points, including any of the following: *Positive* – • It could bring them all closer together • They will probably feel a lot of love for their sons, and be happy to see them develop • Louise may be physically active doing things with the boys • They may be happy that Harry gets the care he needs • Louise and the boys will form a very strong attachment • Louise may be pleased her sons are with her all day, rather than a stranger • They could grow closer to their extended family if they help out with the care *Negative* – • It could put a lot of extra strain on their relationship • They may be so busy with Harry that they don't have time to go out socialising • Louise may feel the boys rely on her too much • They may blame themselves for their son's disability • Louise may get anxious that she is doing something wrong, not doing enough, or that she prioritises Harry over James • Louise may feel annoyed that David wasn't the one to have to give up work • It could be emotionally draining • Because Harry needs permanent care, this could prevent them having a sex life • Louise may feel angry that she had to	(1 mark) x (10 points made)	(10)

		give up work		
		• Louise may miss adult conversation because she is with children all day		
		• They will have less money as there's only one household income, which may stress them out if they're poor		
		• They may feel jealous of parents whose children don't have epilepsy		
		Total marks for question 1		**(30)**

Question		Expected answers	Marks Distribution	Total
2	(a)	*Lifestyle:* the choices someone makes about how they live their life, including diet, exercise, hobbies, smoking, drinking, drugs, and to some extent, their job, housing, family and friends.	(2 marks) for full explanation	(2)
	(b)*	For full marks, candidates should identify a range of positive and negative points for at least two areas of development: Physical: • *Positive* – it could relax her physically and help her wind down / de-stress her • *Negative* – it could cause lung cancer, bronchitis, asthma and other conditions associated with smoking Intellectual: • *Positive* – it could allow her to escape from the intellectual stresses of caring for children; she can contemplate things she couldn't otherwise • *Negative* – it could cause psychological dependence, and she could develop psychoses or paranoia Social: • *Positive* – she could make friends with others who smoke, and socialise more • *Negative* – she could become socially isolated from others, and become detached from her own children Emotional: • *Positive* – it could make her more happy, bubbly and relaxed	(1 mark) x (6 points made)	(6)

		• *Negative* – she could become irritable when not smoking it, and find it harder to bond with her children; she may feel she is addicted to it		
(c) *		Any **three** points fully explained, including any of the following: *Diet* – She should stop eating food which is high in fat and salt, and instead she should eat a balanced diet, including 5 portions of fruit and vegetables per day. She should eat three regular meals and not graze throughout the day. *Exercise* – Annabel does not get any exercise from her job, so she should do it in her spare time. She should take up something simple at first such as swimming or brisk walking, and work up to cardiovascular exercise when she is fitter. *Smoking* – She should give up smoking altogether. She should do this by getting nicotine patches and joining support groups until she is certain that she has stopped it altogether. This will improve her lungs and heart, and possibly her mood swings as well. *Job* – If possible, Annabel should change her job, so that she is doing something more physically and mentally challenging. This would give her exercise and it could therefore improve her self-esteem. If she can get more money this will enable her to move out of the council house and to a better area.	(3-4 marks) x (3 points explained)	(10)
(d)*		For full marks, candidates must show a clear understanding of nature and nurture, and why it is useful. *Nature* – things genetically inherited from one's parents, which cannot be changed. *Nurture* – things that are a result of lifestyle, environment, or social experience; many of these things can be changed by the individual.	(12 marks) for a full, balanced discussion	(12)

	<ul><li>In Annabel's case, she may have inherited a predisposition towards being overweight, or craving foods that are bad for you. In turn, her children may also have this.</li><li>This would be useful for her to know, as then she will be able to work against her instincts to eat badly, in order to maintain a sensible weight.</li><li>Annabel must recognise that even if she has inherited a predisposition towards gaining weight, her lifestyle must be at least partially to blame.</li><li>She eats badly, smokes, and doesn't do any exercise. It is likely that her children have seen this lifestyle choice, and do the same.</li><li>Annabel's weight is likely to have resulted from both nature and nurture, but she can certainly improve it if she makes different lifestyle choices.</li><li>It is useful for her to understand nature and nurture, to see what inherited traits can be overcome through adopting a healthy lifestyle.</li></ul>		
Total marks for question 2			**(30)**

Question			Expected answers	Marks	
				Distribution	Total
3	(a)	(i)	Any one of the following: <ul><li>By 2010 there will be about 870,000 people with dementia in the UK</li><li>In 2050 there will be 1.8 million people with dementia in the UK</li></ul>	(1 mark) x (1 point made)	(1)
		(ii)*	If someone doesn't keep their mind active, it could cause their mental capacities to deteriorate more quickly than if they'd been intellectually stimulated. Additionally, we now have better medical care which keeps people alive for longer (it's more common in old age)	(2 marks) for full explanation	(2)
		(iii)*	Someone may inherit a predisposition towards getting dementia in later life – this may go hand	(2 marks) for full	(2)

		in hand with a genetic predisposition for longevity (it's most common in very old people)	explanation	
(b) *		Candidates should identify **two** factors affecting attitudes, including any of the following: • The more common it gets, the more society gets used to it and accepts it • Putting people with dementia into mental hospitals labels them negatively • Seeing more people with dementia could scare people; they might realise they could get it when they are older • If people do not know anyone with dementia then they may not fully understand it • People may find it funny that people with dementia do and say strange things	(2 marks) x (2 points explained)	(4)
(c)		*Positive definition:* Being fit, feeling well, and having a normal weight, blood pressure, Body Mass Index, etc. For example, someone who eats a balanced diet, exercises and has normal blood pressure and body size. The positive definition focuses on the presence of physical evidence, rather than someone's emotions, relationships, etc.	(3 marks) for full explanation	(3)
(d) *		For full marks, candidates must explain **five** aims, including any of the following: • To encourage people to do more exercise • To get people to eat a balanced diet, including five portions of fruit and vegetables per day • To make people understand the causes of illnesses • To help people to understand how health problems can be treated or prevented • To inform people about the available health strategies or services • To get overweight people to lose weight • To encourage people to give up smoking • To get people immunised against common infections and diseases	(2 marks) x (5 points explained)	(10)

		• To encourage sensible consumption of alcohol		
(e) *		For full marks, candidates must explain **one** negative effect on each area of development, including any of the following: Physical: • It can cause a physical addiction • Veins can collapse if drugs are injected • If drugs are snorted, it can damage the lining of the nose • Can cause heart problems • It harms the baby in pregnant women • Smoking drugs can cause many cancers Intellectual: • People can develop psychoses and mental conditions • People may have blackouts, flashbacks, or memory loss • Many drugs can be psychologically addictive • People may be unable to cope effectively with education or learning new things Social: • People can become isolated from family and friends • Someone's attitudes or personality may change Emotional: • Someone can become panicky, paranoid, depressed, or anxious • The 'come down' may be dreadful	(2 marks) x (4 points explained)	(8)
		Total marks for Question 3		**(30)**
		TOTAL MARKS FOR EXAMINATION PAPER		**(90)**

Completed Exams

In this section you will find two completed examination papers (Sample Examination #1). *"Candidate A"* is a weak student, who would achieve approximately a grade C, whereas *"Candidate B"* is a very strong candidate who would get a grade A.

Look at the examiner's comments in the margin; these will tell you why marks have or haven't been awarded. Being able to tell the difference between a good answer and a poor answer brings you one step closer to being able to get a good grade in the examination.

CANDIDATE A

Answer ALL questions in the spaces provided

1

Adam is 6, and his brother, Sam is three years old: they live with their mother, Shannon. They are both growing and developing normally for their age. Adam enjoys football and he plays it in an after-school club once a week. The children's father lived with Shannon until two years ago; he has now moved abroad and has a new wife.

(a) Explain the difference between growth and development.

Growth is getting taller. Developement is emotional, social or interlectual, for example a child growes bigger and then he can run around and make friends. Children need to develope so that they can get jobs and do well in school when there older. } ···*Vague and irrelevant*

(4)   *1*

Vague on development

Leave
blank

Answer ALL questions in the spaces provided

Adam is 6, and his brother, Sam is three years old: they live with their mother, Shannon. They are both growing and developing normally for their age. Adam enjoys football and he plays it in an after-school club once a week. The children's father lived with Shannon until two years ago; he has now moved abroad and has a new wife.

(a) Explain the difference between growth and development.

Growth is a physical increase in size or weight, e.g. growing ✓

taller or heavier. Development is an increase in skills or ✓

abilities. These skills can be physical, intellectual, social or ✓

emotional. For example, an infant develops socially

because he forms an attachment to his mother or father,

and can differentiate between parents and strangers, but
at birth, he was unable to do this. ✓

(4)

4

*Good, full
answer*

CANDIDATE A

Leave blank

(b) Identify **two** factors that could affect Adam's physical development.

The food he eats ✓ will effect wether he gets fat or not, but he could get around this by excercising. His school will effect his developement as it will teach him new things. And his parents will effect him because they might tell him off alot. **?**

1

Three factors identified

(2)

(c) Discuss how Adam's development might be affected by playing football.

- He will get fitter because of all the runing about ✓ *(Phys +)*
- He will be healthier ⟵
- He enjoys playing football ✓ *(Emo +)*
- He will loose weight ⟵
- He might get injurred ✓ *(Phys -)*
- He will make friends with other boys ✓ *(Soc +)*
- He will have fun

No marks available, as one positive physical thing has already been identified

Repeated

4

Doesn't cover all areas of development

(8)

Leave blank

(b) Identify **two** factors that could affect Adam's physical development.

1. Adam's physical development will be affected by his parents - e.g. if they praise him when he learns new physical skills, he'll want to progress more. ✓

2. Adam's school will affect his physical development because if they offer a good range of sports, Adam can find one that he enjoys which will improve his co-ordination. ✓ **(2)**

2
Clearly explained

(c) Discuss how Adam's development might be affected by playing football.

PHYS+   He will get fitter and healthier from the exercise, developing muscle tone, stamina, speed and his ball skills ✓

PHYS -   He may get tired from all the running about, or get muscle strains from working too hard ✓

INT +   He will have to learn how the scoring system works which could help his maths ✓

INT -   He may find the rules confusing and not be able to understand them ✓

EMO +   He will have lots of fun playing the game ✓

EMO -   He might get very upset if his team loses a match ✓

SOC +   He may make lots of new friends with the other team members, and develop his teamwork skills ✓

SOC -   He might get bullied by the other players if he scores an own goal or plays badly ✓

(8)

8
Balanced answer for all 4 areas

CANDIDATE A

Leave blank

(d) Sam is meeting the norms expected of a boy his age. Explain what is meant by 'norms'.

Norms are the normal stages that people go threw in there life, ✓

No marks for listing!

e.g. ✓

like learning to speak, learning to walk, learning to go to

school, the learning how to made friends, with other people, and

learning how to follow instructions given by there teachers.

The norms are what normal people go threw.

2
Vague

(4)

(e) Explain how a child's intellectual development will progress during infancy.

Infancy is the life stage from birth to 2 years old. Children

learn lots of things during infancy, like they learn how to put

shapes in puzzles and how to reconise colours, and reconise

✗ *Emo*

that there mum loves them and they form a attachmeant to

there mum. They learn how to speak and say words and

sentences to there parents. ✓

1
Very confused

(4)

Leave blank

(d) Sam is meeting the norms expected of a boy his age. Explain what is meant by 'norms'.

Norms are the average milestones that are expected of all people at a certain age; these can be growth or developmental norms. Norms progress in an expected pattern, each skill building on the last, e.g. an infant will walk before he runs. Norms are fairly universal all across the world, but even if someone doesn't reach a norm, this doesn't mean they're 'abnormal'. **(4)**

4 *Full, good answer*

(e) Explain how a child's intellectual development will progress during infancy.

During infancy, an enormous amount of intellectual development takes place. E.g. at birth an infant doesn't understand any language, but by the age of 2, they confidently speak around 200 words. They can often learn far faster than adults can - especially with language. Infants learn by modelling or copying adults and older children. By age 2 they will be able to complete simple puzzles such as fitting shapes into the right holes **(4)**

4 *Well-explained*

CANDIDATE A

Leave blank

(e) Discuss how Adam and Sam's development could be affected by not having a father in their lives.

- They might miss their farther and wish he was still around ✓ *(Emo +)*

- They might descide that they want to find him when they grown up. ✗ *irrelevant*

- They might love there mother more because she's all they've got ✓ *(Soc +)*

- They might get bullied. ✓ *(Soc -)*

- They might get a new step farther who they don't like. ✗ *irrelevant*

3
Basic understanding

(8)

(Total 30 marks)

12

CANDIDATE B

(e) Discuss how Adam and Sam's development could be affected by not having a father in their lives.

PHYS + They might be more physically adept if they have had to take on household tasks such as washing up or basic DIY ✓

PHYS - They might miss out on playing physical games such as football, if their mum can't play football ✓

INT + They may develop their language very quickly because they are always able to talk to their mum, rather than having to share her with their dad ✓

INT - They might struggle with homework if their mum can't help them because she is always so busy with housework ✓

EMO + They may be really happy that they've got their mum and they are a close family ✓

EMO - They might feel upset that their dad has abandoned them ✓

SOC + They might fit in well if lots of their friends also live in single parent households ✓

SOC - They may not understand gender roles or that the role of a father is ✓

8

Clear, balanced argument

(8)

(Total 30 marks)

30

CANDIDATE A

Leave blank

2 Gerald is 59 and is about to retire from his job as the Managing Director of a haulage company. Gerald's wife divorced him four years ago, after she discovered that she was homosexual; she now lives with her female partner. Gerald tries to eat sensibly, and he has recently started going swimming again, which he is good at and enjoys.

(a) What life stage is Gerald in?

Adulthood ✗

(1)   *0*
        Imprecise

(b) Gerald is fully mature. Explain what 'maturation' is.

Maturation is when your mature and you become more

sensible and don't make silly descisions. It happens when you

get older, e.g. over 18. children are very imature and they

don't understand very much, but mature people are much more

sensible. ✗   *Confused, irrelevant*

(3)   *0*
        Very
        confused

(c) Identify **three** effects of ageing that Gerald may be noticing in himself.

Grey hair ✓

Wrinkles ✓

Going mad ✗

(3)   *2*
        Basic

Leave blank

2 Gerald is 59 and is about to retire from his job as the Managing Director of a haulage company. Gerald's wife divorced him four years ago, after she discovered that she was homosexual; she now lives with her female partner. Gerald tries to eat sensibly, and he has recently started going swimming again, which he is good at and enjoys.

(a) What life stage is Gerald in?

Middle adulthood. ✓

1

(1)

(b) Gerald is fully mature. Explain what 'maturation' is.

Maturation is a body clock that is genetically pre-programmed from birth. ✓ It tells your body when to go through puberty, when to have the menopause, ✓ etc. Maturation occurs in all people regardless of any social or environmental triggers ✓ - e.g. you get pubic hair whether or not you attend school.

3

Good, full answer

(3)

(c) Identify **three** effects of ageing that Gerald may be noticing in himself.

1. His hair will probably be going grey ✓

2. He will probably have less stamina when exercising, than he used to when he was a young man ✓

3. He will probably be getting wrinkles around his eyes and mouth ✓

3

Clear knowledge shown

(3)

CANDIDATE A

Leave blank

(d) Gerald describes himself as middle class. Discuss how belonging to the middle classes can affect someone's physical, intellectual, social and emotional development.

Being middle class is good because it means you have more money, you can spend this on things like nice hollidays, and going out for meals with friends, ✓ *(Soc +)* and you might be able to give up work if you have enough money. You have to have a good job to be middle class, and that way you'll earn a good wage. ✓ *(Emo +)* You will be happy emotionaly because you have lots of money and nice clothes and posessions and it will help your social development because you will have lots of time and money to socialise. You can go to places like expensive restaraunts and join expensive sports and hobbies like chess or gambling. You might have lots of new friends you didn't have before but you can't be sure if they really like you or just not because there shallow.

Confused

(8)

2

Repetitive, narrow focus

Leave
blank

(d) Gerald describes himself as middle class. Discuss how belonging to the middle classes can affect someone's physical, intellectual, social and emotional development.

PHYS + Middle class people tend to eat a better diet than working class people, with more fruit and veg, and less saturated fat and salt ✓

PHYS - Middle class people with office jobs may be less physically fit than someone who does a manual job, because the office workers don't get any exercise as part of their job. ✓

INT + In GCSEs and A-Levels, middle class people tend to achieve better than working class people ✓

INT - Middle class teenagers may be pressured into doing A-Levels or attending university by their parents, who also went to university ✓

EMO + Middle class people are probably very happy if they have lots of money to buy anything they want ✓

EMO - They might be unhappy if they think people only like them for their money ✓   (8)

SOC + They may have lots of money to go out socialising and be very popular ✓

SOC - They may not have much time to go out socialising if ✓ they have a high powered job that takes up a lot of time

8
Full,
balanced
answer

119

CANDIDATE A

Leave blank

(e) Explain **three** ways in which swimming could positively affect Gerald's physical development.

1 It will help his mussles get stronger, because all that exercise
will build mussles instead of fat. This is good because then he
will be stronger and he will look good, and it could stop him
ageing badly and looking really old ~ No marks for 2nd point

basic

2 It will also help his lungs because you breath alot when your
swimming and that is good for your lungs.

vague

3 He will get fit. This is important because if your fit then
your not fat, and this is important because lots of people are
obease these days and they eat to much food and don't
excercise.

Not explained enough

(10)

3

Vague, repetitive

Leave
blank

(e) Explain **three** ways in which swimming could positively affect Gerald's physical development.

1 Gerald's cardiovascular system will be improved, as swimming makes your heart work harder and you breathe more heavily. His heart will become strengthened and his lung capacity may improve if he holds his breath a lot under water. When you do a lot of cardiovascular activity, it becomes easier to do cardiovascular activity in the future.

2 Gerald's muscles will improve and get stronger. At this age, he may be suffering muscle wastage, and swimming will slow this down, or even build stronger muscles. Swimming quickly requires strong muscles, so if Gerald swims quickly then his muscles will improve their strength and stamina. He may notice that his limbs feel more toned.

3 Gerald will strengthen his joints by swimming. Joints can get stiffer or uncomfortable in older people, but doing regular exercise like swimming will decrease the likelihood of this, and prevent them from being painful. This will be especially true of his shoulder, hip and knee joints which are used a great deal in swimming.

(10)

10
Fully
explained

CANDIDATE A

Leave blank

(e) Gerald has five grandchildren, whom he sees every weekend, and they have all been socialised since a young age. Explain the importance of early socialisation in children.

No marks available

Socialization is when you mix with other people to learn how to act. You can do this in the family, or with friends, or in a school or when you have a job. It's when you go out with friends and have fun together then your socialising. This helps build friendships and then you will be happy, because a people of all ages like to have friends, and if you don't have any friends then you will be upset and get bullied.

(5)

1

Doesn't explain the importance of it

(Total 30 marks)

8

Leave blank

(e) Gerald has five grandchildren, whom he sees every weekend, and they have all been socialised since a young age. Explain the importance of early socialisation in children.

Socialisation is important as it allows children to mix with others to learn social norms and customs. This is vital in infancy and early childhood because without it, children cannot know the normal ways to interact with people. Simple things like manners, turn-taking, sharing and friendships can only be learned through socialisation, and without these skills people will find it very hard to progress socially in later life. They may be unable to make friends, **(5)** or they might get bullied for acting oddly, **(Total 30 marks)** and this could go on to give them a negative self-concept.

5

Clear, full answer

30

CANDIDATE A

Leave blank

3   Governments, charities, and other organisations often run health promotion campaigns. The following information was published by the charity Cancer Research UK.

> **<u>Lung Cancer and Smoking Statistics</u>**
>
> Tobacco consumption is recognised as the UK's single greatest cause of preventable illness and early death, with more than 120,000 people dying each year from smoking-related diseases. Around 90% of lung cancer cases in the UK are caused by tobacco smoking. In Britain the highest rates of smoking are in the 20-24 age-group, with 37% of men and 38% of women this age recorded as smokers. The number of people who smoke regularly has been declining steadily since the 1950s, but there are still around 13 million adult cigarette smokers in Great Britain. A further 2 million adults smoke pipes and/or cigars.

Source: Cancer Research UK, 2004

(a) From the information given, identify **one** piece of evidence which suggests that smoking is a significant problem in the UK.

It's the biggest cause of preventable illnes's ✓

1

(1)

(b) Health can be defined in a number of different ways. Three ways are holistically, positively, and negatively. Explain what is meant by the holistic definition of health.

The holistic definition of health looks at all factors of a

persons life, like there diet, excercise, smoking, drinking,

drugs, health, job, and they're hobby's. ✓ it looks at things like

there physical, emotional, social and interlectual well being. ✓

(3)   **2**

Incomplete

Leave blank

3   Governments, charities, and other organisations often run health promotion campaigns. The following information was published by the charity Cancer Research UK.

> ### Lung Cancer and Smoking Statistics
>
> Tobacco consumption is recognised as the UK's single greatest cause of preventable illness and early death, with more than 120,000 people dying each year from smoking-related diseases. Around 90% of lung cancer cases in the UK are caused by tobacco smoking. In Britain the highest rates of smoking are in the 20-24 age-group, with 37% of men and 38% of women this age recorded as smokers. The number of people who smoke regularly has been declining steadily since the 1950s, but there are still around 13 million adult cigarette smokers in Great Britain. A further 2 million adults smoke pipes and/or cigars.

Source: Cancer Research UK, 2004

(a)   From the information given, identify **one** piece of evidence which suggests that smoking is a significant problem in the UK.

It's the greatest cause of preventable illness and early death ✓

(1)   *1*

(b)   Health can be defined in a number of different ways. Three ways are holistically, positively, and negatively. Explain what is meant by the holistic definition of health.

Holistic definition: not just the absence of illness or disease,

but total physical, intellectual, social, emotional and

spiritual wellbeing. ✓ *This covers all aspects of a person's life,*

including their weight, diet, habits, their mental state,

their relationships, and their self-concept. ✓ *E.g. even if a*

person with schizophrenia can run a long way without   (3)   *3*

getting tired, they are still not "healthy" because of their

impaired mental state. ✓

Clearly and fully explained

125

CANDIDATE A

Leave blank

(b) Health promotion campaigns can be approached in different ways, including:
- the biomedical approach
- the educational / behaviour approach
- the societal change approach

(i) Explain **four** potential barriers to the success of an educational / behavioural health promotion campaign.

1 A education. / behavioural campaign is where the health campaign focus's on giving people information so that they will change the things they do. Eg. a TV advert

not a barrier

2 One problems with a TV advert is that not everyone watches TV, maybe they go out to the pub or do sports or read books instead. ✓

Not enough explanation

3 Leaflets are thrown away alot expecially when there given out in the town, people just throw them away with out looking at them. ✓

vague

4 TV adverts are sometimes boring or complicated so people don't watch them because they don't like them if there not eye-catchy. ✓

vague

(8)

3

Confused, little explanation

(b) Health promotion campaigns can be approached in different ways, including:
- the biomedical approach
- the educational / behaviour approach
- the societal change approach

(i) Explain **four** potential barriers to the success of an educational / behavioural health promotion campaign.

1 *TV documentaries are often ignored because people* ✓ *don't want to watch them: the people who do watch them probably don't need helping. If the campaign doesn't reach the target audience, it can't help them.* ✓

2 *Poster or billboard campaigns are often not noticed -* *motorists can only glance at them, so they may miss* ✓ *what the advert is trying to show, and therefore won't change their behaviour because of it.* ✓

3 *School talks are not very effective because teenagers* *don't like being told what to do by adults, so they might* ✓ *rebel against anything they are told, and do the opposite.* ✓

4 *Website campaigns are probably unsuccessful because* *people don't search for them and they don't just discover* *them by chance, so they may not even know the* ✓ *campaign was there.* ✓

(8)

8
Four points
explained
well

127

CANDIDATE A

Leave blank

(ii) Discuss the possible success of an anti-smoking campaign which uses a societal change approach.

No marks – not evaluative

A social change campaign. Is one where they change the law to make it so that everyone has to obide by the law. For example a law saying you can't smoke if your under 18 is a social change campaign law. This would work well because people listen if it's the law and if it's on television then they know about it being a new law and don't do it. ✓

But some people will do it anyway because of peer pressure and the law can't stop that ✓ also not everyone obides by the law ✓ because they think its cool to break the law or they can just get there friend to bye them cigarettes or find a shop where they will sell them to them even if there not old

Repeated

enough. ✓ So social change doesn't really work on smoking because people ignore the law and just do it anyway with friends because it's fun and cool.

4
Vague basic

(10)

Leave blank

(ii) Discuss the possible success of an anti-smoking campaign which uses a societal change approach.

+ Many people abide by the law and try not to break it ✓

+ Parents would put extra pressure on teenagers if e.g. the smoking age is raised to 18 instead of 16 ✓

+ It would make people listen and think more about how dangerous something is, if it's illegal it must be bad

+ If the law was publicised on television, newspapers, etc. then everyone would know about the law change, and cohere with it ✓

- Lots of 15-year-olds already buy cigarettes easily, so raising the age to 18 won't stop most teenagers from still buying cigarettes ✓

- Teenagers especially like to ignore the law, and to rebel against it for fun ✓

- It wouldn't help teenagers who are already addicted

- It would be better to have some behavioural therapy as well as a law change.

- If the smoking age was raised, lots of shops might ignore the law and try to make more money ✓

- It might be hard to enforce a new law ✓

- A law (e.g.) banning smoking in public places can't (10) tackle the people who just smoke in private ✓

- If smoking was made completely illegal (like drugs) then it would just push it into the back streets ✓

10

Good, balanced, range of points

CANDIDATE A

Leave blank

(d)   Describe **one** negative effect on each area of development caused by smoking:

Physical: People who smoke get lung cancer and mouth cancer and bronchitis, from all the nicotine that goes into there lungs

More than one effect, confused

Intellectual: People may think they are going to try and give up, but then they don't so they get angry about wether there giving up or not but they don't know

Very confused

Social: People enjoy smoking socially if lots of there friends smoke then they can all smoke together and make friends that way

Not a negative effect

Emotional: People might feel upset if they try and give up but don't, so they just carry on smoking but they feel guilty about it because they were going to give up but then didn't.

Confused

(8)

1

Very confused

| (Total 30 marks) | 11 |

TOTAL FOR PAPER: 90 marks

31

Leave blank

(d)   Describe **one** negative effect on each area of development caused by smoking:

Physical: Lung cancer is often the result of smoking. This involves tumours growing in the lungs, making it hard to breathe. This cancer might spread to other areas of the body and ultimately kill the person. ✓

Intellectual: People might not be able to concentrate on things if they are desperate for a cigarette - e.g. a lorry driver who is not allowed to smoke in his lorry may not be able to fully pay attention to the road, which is dangerous ✓

Social: Non-smokers might not want to be friends with a person who smokes if they really hate the smell of smoke. So the person who smokes might lose a lot of friends who don't want their clothes and hair to smell of cigarettes. ✓

Emotional: Most smokers want to give up, and they may feel very upset or annoyed with themselves if they can't give up smoking. It takes a lot of willpower and some people may just be too weak-willed and unable to give up. So they may feel guilty with themselves for not being able to give up. ✓   (8)

8
Clear,
accurate

(Total 30 marks)   30

TOTAL FOR PAPER: 90 marks

90

Glossary

This section contains an alphabetised list of all the terminology you may not be familiar with. All words which are highlighted in **bold** throughout the Fast Facts section can be found here in the Glossary, with their definitions. Words in *italics* in this section can be found elsewhere in the Glossary

You should make sure you know what all these words mean before you attempt a Sample Examination Paper. When sitting the exam, try to use the correct terminology as outlined in this section: it impresses the examiners if you can use such terms in your answers.

GLOSSARY

Abstract thinking — The ability to think about hypothetical situations or concepts, planning ahead and asking *rhetorical questions*

Adulthood — The time from 19 years of age onwards; often split into *Early adulthood* (19 to 45 years), *Middle adulthood* (45 to 65 years) and *Later adulthood / old age* (65 years onwards)

Agility — Being able to change direction or activity with speed and precision – e.g. when running or doing an assault course

Alzheimer's disease — The most common form of *dementia*, characterised by memory loss and declining mental capabilities

Associative play — When children play alongside one another, and may take an interest in what each other is doing, but they don't play <u>with</u> each other

Attachment — A strong emotional bond; a feeling of love formed between a baby and a carer (usually the mother or father)

Axillary hair — Another name for hair which grows under the arms

Bilingual — Being able to speak two languages fluently

Binge drinking — Drinking half the recommended weekly allowance of alcohol over a short period of time (e.g. a few hours)

Biomedical — Approach to health promotion to do with visible symptoms and illnesses; changing the health of people through medical practices like immunisation or screening

Body Mass Index (BMI) — A way of measuring whether a person is a healthy weight for their height. A healthy BMI is 20 to 25.

Campaign — A way in which people try to change the health of others, e.g. through TV adverts, injections, posters, or changes in the law

Cardiovascular — Type of exercise which makes your heart beat faster and your breathing harder

Centile chart — A graph showing the average height or weight of people of certaint ages, usually with the 5th and 95th centiles (percentages) shown

Childhood — The *life stage* from 2 to 8 years old

Chromosome — The microscopically tiny, X-shaped structures that exist in pairs in the nucleus of every living cell. They contain all the *DNA* and *genes* coiled up hundreds of thousands of times

Circle of deprivation — Being born into a poor family, and staying poor because you can't escape *poverty*

Class — Someone's wealth, education, socio-economic status or job status

Class A drug — Types of drugs that are extremely dangerous: heroin, cocaine, crack, ecstasy, LSD, magic mushrooms

Class B drugs — Very dangerous drugs, but which aren't as bad as Class A drugs: amphetamines, methylphenidate (ritalin), pholcodine

Class C drugs — Drugs that are dangerous, but not as much as Class B drugs: cannabis, tranquilisers, some painkillers, gamma hydroxybutyrate (GHB), ketamine

Cognitive — To do with knowledge, intellect, or the mind

Conditioning — A way of learning something, where a child or animal repeats behaviour that is rewarded, and stops behaviour that is punished or ignored

Co-operative play — When children play <u>with</u> one another, rather than just <u>near</u> one another

Decentring — The ability to see things from other people's point of view (the opposite of being *egocentric*)

Dementia — The decline of mental function, most commonly seen in elderly people

Depressants — Drugs which dull your senses and make you feel very calm and relaxed, e.g. cannabis and heroin (note- depressants do <u>not</u> make you depressed!)

Development — An increase in skills or abilities; the physical, intellectual, emotional and social changes that occur in a person

DNA — Short for Deoxyribo-Nucleic Acid. The double-helix (twisted ladder) shaped molecules that are made up of the four *nucleotide bases*

Dominant — Of a *gene*, one that 'takes control' over *recessive* genes, and determines characteristics

Dysfunction — Abnormal or impaired functioning of something

Early adulthood — The *life stage* from 19 to 45 years old

Ectopic pregnancy — When the fertilised egg, rather than embedding in the uterus and developing normally, embeds itself in the fallopian tube: ectopic pregnancies always miscarry or have to be terminated

Egocentric — Only being concerned with your emotions and yourself (infants up to the age of 3 ish)

Endocrine glands — Parts of the body that release *hormones*

Fine motor skill — A physical ability using the small muscles of the hands, e.g. writing, grasping, sewing

Foetus — Unborn baby, as it grows in the womb for nine months

Gamete — A sex cell: either a sperm cell produced in males, or an egg cell (*ovum*) produced in females

Gender constancy — Understanding that one's sex is fixed, and does not alter with the passage of time

Gene — A section of *DNA* that has a particular function – e.g. to give the bearer blue eyes. It is the sequence of our genes that makes us unique

Genotype — The full set of *chromosomes*, containing all the physical information to make a human being

Gestation — The nine-month period of foetal development, during which a baby grows in the womb

Global warming — Also called the greenhouse effect: increase in the average temperature of the earth

Gonadotropic hormones — Sexual *hormones*, released from the testes in boys, or ovaries in girls

Greenhouse effect — see *Global warming*

Gross motor skill — A physical ability using the big muscles of the body, e.g. walking, throwing, kicking

Growth — The physical increase in the size and weight of a person

Hallucinogens — Drugs which make you see or hear things that aren't there, e.g. acid, magic mushrooms

Health — Lack of disease; feeling well, happy and normal

Health promotion — Trying to get people to be more fit and healthy through various *campaigns*

Hereditary — A characteristic which is inherited through *genes* from your parents, e.g. nose shape, skin colour, hair curliness

Holistic — "Wholeness": an approach to health that includes all types of wellbeing (physical, intellectual, social, emotional, financial, spiritual, etc.)

Holophrase — One word which is used in different ways to mean different things, e.g. "dada" can mean "where is daddy?" or "hello daddy!"

Hormones — Chemicals released by the body to make the body do something, e.g. grow, develop sexually

Immunisation — Injections to protect against illnesses such as measles, mumps, rubella and tuberculosis

Infancy — The *life stage* from 0 – 2 years old

Innate reflex — An instinct which is in-built from birth; things like sucking and grasping (also known as primitive reflexes)

Inverse law — When the people who need something the most (e.g. elderly people needing health care) are the ones with the least access to it

Later adulthood — The *life stage* from 65 years onwards (also known as old age)

Life course — The unique series of events that go together to make up one person's life

Life expectancy — The average age at which people die; the amount of time it is predicted that a particular person has left to live

Life span — The actual duration of time from a person's birth until their death

Life stage — The six age groups that people can be separated into: *Infancy, childhood, adolescence, early adulthood, middle adulthood* and *later adulthood* (old age)

Lifestyle — The unique way a person chooses to live; their diet, exercise, smoking and drinking habits, job, hobbies and interests

Linguistic — To do with language. The 'linguistic stage' is when someone says words with meanings attached to them

Locomotive skills — *Motor skills* that allow one to move around, e.g. crawling, walking, running, skipping (also known as locomotor skills)

Manipulative skills — *Fine motor skills;* movements of the small muscles in the hands and fingers, to handle objects

Manual dexterity — Small, precise movements, often of the hands, to manipulate small objects

Maturation — A 'body clock' which tells the body when to start menstruating, when to get grey hair, etc

Maturity — The state of being fully developed physically and mentally

Menarche — A girl's first period / menstrual cycle

Menopause — The shutting down of the body's reproductive system (in women) at 45 to 50 years of age

Meritocracy — A society where your class, job, or wealth is determined by individual merit (i.e. your skills) rather than by what class you were born into

Middle adulthood — The life stage from 45 – 65 years old

Modelling — When babies or children copy the behaviour of adults and older children

Morbidity — Illness: morbidity rates are illness rates

Mortality — Death: mortality rates are death rates

Motor skill — The ability to move your own body in a controlled way

Multilingual — Being able to speak three or more languages fluently

Nature — (As in the nature / nurture debate): Unchangeable *genes*, inherited from one's parents

Norms — Average milestones that are expected in all individuals at a certain age – e.g. to start walking at 12 months of age

Noxious substances — Substances or chemicals that are harmful, poisonous or dangerous to humans

Nuclear family — A married man and woman and their children

Nucleotide — Nucleotide bases are four chemicals (Adenine, Guanine, Thymine, Cytosine) which form the 'rungs' of the double-helix ladder in *DNA*. They always bond (A-T) and (G-C)

Nurture — (As in the nature / nurture debate): Experience and learning since birth

Nutrients — Substances found in foods – e.g. fat, carbohydrate, protein

Nutrition — Eating food and absorbing *nutrients* from it, like vitamins, minerals, carbohydrates, fat

Obesity — The state of being grossly overweight; having a *BMI* above 30

Object permanence — Understanding that an object continues to exist even if it has been covered up or moved away

Oestrogen — Female sex *hormone* responsible for the *secondary sexual characteristics* in females

Old age — The life stage from 65 years onwards, also known as *later adulthood*

Ovulation — Production of eggs in the reproductive system (ovaries)

Ovum — The egg cell, released each month in women

Parallel play — When children play by imitating adults or other children

Passive smoking — Breathing in other people's cigarette or tobacco smoke

Peer group / peers — People who all share something in common, usually age, gender and culture

Peer pressure — Strong encouragement from one's friends or age group to do something

Pester power — When children see something (e.g. on television) and then pester and beg their parents to buy it for them

Political correctness (PC) — Using acceptable language that is not racist, sexist, homophobic, offensive, etc.

Pollution — Contamination of the environment with materials that affect human health, quality of life, or the natural functioning of ecosystems

Positive discrimination — Employing a certain percentage or number of ethnic minority people, or disabled people

Postcode lottery — A method of deciding whether a patient can have certain medical treatment, based on the postcode of their house

Poverty — Being extremely poor

Prejudice — An unfair idea about certain groups of people, often based on people's looks – e.g. he must be a criminal because he's black

Pre-linguistic — The noises a baby makes before being able to say words with meanings: instead, they babble meaningless sounds "babababa"

Pressure group — A group of people who try to change society, through demonstrations or posters / leaflets e.g. anti-smoking campaigners; anti-abortion groups; environmental associations

Primary sexual characteristics — Sexual traits that are present from birth e.g. vagina, ovaries

Primary socialisation — In the family, children learn how to interact with others and acquire values

Primitive reflex — An instinct which is in-built from birth; things like sucking and grasping (also known as *innate reflexes*)

Progesterone — Female sex hormone responsible for the *secondary sexual characteristics* in females

Puberty — The time during which *secondary sexual characteristics* develop (approximately 11 – 16 years of age)

Recessive — Of a *gene*, one which can only determine characteristics if a *dominant* one isn't present

Rehabilitation — Helping people to get back to normal after an addiction, illness or disability

Respiratory — To do with breathing; asthma and bronchitis are respiratory problems

Rhetorical questions — "Big" questions which may not have an answer; "why are we here?" "what is it that makes me me?"

Role strain — When somebody has too many roles (mother, worker, carer, cook) to cope with them all

Sanitation — Promoting health by getting rid of germs and waste, e.g. through a sewage system

Screening — Scans that check for illnesses or conditions, e.g. breast cancer scans, smear tests

Secondary sexual characteristics — Sexual traits that develop during or after *puberty* e.g. menstruation

Secondary socialisation — In schools or other gatherings, children learn how to behave in public or among strangers

Self-concept — Your idea of yourself, including physical, intellectual, emotional and social ideas

Sensori-motor — (or sensory motor) Development and learning through the senses and physical movement

Social class — see *Class*

Social exclusion — Having far fewer opportunities than others; not feeling a part of mainstream society

Social mobility — The possibility for someone to change their class (ideally for the better)

Social role — The expected behaviour of someone, e.g. mother, carer, teenager, older person

Socialisation — Mixing with other people, so as to learn how to interact with others

Stamina — The ability to keep going for a long time – e.g. to run a marathon

State Benefits — Money given to poor people and other disadvantaged groups from the government. For example, Income Support, Tax Credits, Jobseekers Allowance, Disability Living Allowance

Stereotype — An (often inaccurate) assumption that everyone belonging to a certain group are the same as each other: e.g. all Indian people own corner shops

Stigma — Negative ideas or attitudes towards certain people or ways of life

Stimulants — Drugs which give you energy and make you feel wide awake, e.g. speed, cocaine, ecstasy

Substance abuse — Alcohol abuse, drug abuse, or any other substances taken often or irresponsibly

Telegraphic speech — Two-word sentences that are grammatical and have meaning: "daddy gone" "kick ball" "where dolly?"

Testes — Testicles

Testosterone — The male sex *hormone*, responsible for the *secondary sexual characteristics* in males

Values — Morals, ideas and beliefs that a person holds about how to act

Virtuous errors — A child learning to speak correctly applies the rules of language, but makes a few mistakes, e.g. "He teached me", "Two sheeps"

Wet dreams — When a boy ejaculates while he is asleep in bed

Further Reading and Index

The Further Reading section gives you a list of books and websites you may wish to use to broaden your knowledge of certain topics. Any of these resources could be useful when revising for your Human Growth and Development examination.

The Index is given to enable you to find topics quickly and easily.

FURTHER READING

Allott, M. and Robb, M. [Eds] (1997) *Understanding Health and Social Care: An Introductory Reader*, London, SAGE Publications Ltd

Bee, H. L. and Bjorklund, B. L. (2007) *The Journey of Adulthood* [5th Edition], New Jersey, Prentice Hall

Cheridan, M.D., Frost, M. and Sharma, A. (1997) *From Birth to Five Years: Children's Developmental Progress*, Oxford, Routledge (Taylor & Francis)

Clarke, L. (2000) *Health and Social Care for Intermediate GNVQ* [2nd Edition], Cheltenham, Stanley Thornes

Cottrell, S. (2003) *The Study Skills Handbook*, Basingstoke, Palgrave Macmillan

Cottrell, S. (2006) *The Exam Skills Handbook*, Basingstoke, Palgrave Macmillan

Department of Health (1999) *Children's Needs, Parenting Capacity: The Impact of Parental Mental Illness, Problem Alcohol and Drug Use and Domestic Violence on Children's Development*, Norwich, The Stationery Office Books

Dowling. M. (2005) *Young Children's Personal, Social and Emotional Development* [2nd Edition], London, Paul Chapman Publishing

Ewles, L. and Simnett, I. (2003) *Promoting Health: A Practical Guide* [5th Edition], London, Bailliere Tindall

Goodman, H. (2007) *Drink, Drugs and Your Body*, London, Hodder Wayland

Hall, D.M.B. and Elliman, D. (2006) *Health for All Children* [4th Edition], Oxford, Oxford University Press

Howe, D. (2005) *Child Abuse and Neglect: Attachment, Development and Intervention*, Basingstoke, Palgrave Macmillan

Kreitman, T., Finlay, F. and Jones, R. (2001) *Everything You Ever Wanted to Ask About Periods*, London, Piccadilly Press Ltd

Kreitman, T., Simpson, N. and Jones, R. (2002) *Everything You Ever Wanted to Ask About Willies and Other Boys' Bits*, London, Piccadilly Press Ltd

Lindon, J. (2005) *Understanding Child Development: Linking Theory to Practice*, London, Hodder Arnold

Meggitt, C. (2006) *Child Development: An Illustrated Guide* [2nd Edition], Oxford, Heinemann Educational Publishers

Meredith, S. and Gee, R. (1997) *Growing Up (Facts of Life)* [2nd Edition], London, Usborne Publishing Ltd.

Moonie, N. [Ed] (2000) *AVCE Advanced Health and Social Care* [3rd Edition], Oxford, Heinemann Educational Publishers

Moonie, N. (2005) *GCE AS Level in Health and Social Care (for Edexcel) Double Award Book*, Oxford, Heinemann Educational Publishers

Moonie, N. [Ed] (2006) *GCE A2 Level in Health and Social Care (for Edexcel)*, Oxford, Heinemann Educational Publishers

Naidoo, J. and Willis, J. (2004) *Public Health and Health Promotion: Developing Practice* [2nd Edition], Oxford, Bailliere Tindall (Elsevier Books)

Richards, J. (2003) *Complete A-Z Health and Social Care Handbook*, London, Hodder Arnold

Tassoni, P., Beith, K., Eldridge, H. and Gough, A. (2002) *Diploma in Child Care and Education* [3rd Edition], Oxford, Heinemann Educational Publishers

Thomson, A. (2005) *Health and Social Care: AS for EDEXCEL: Resource Pack*, London, Collins Educational

Thomson, H., Aslangul, S., Holden, C. and Meggitt, C. (2000) *Health & Social Care Vocational A-Level* [3rd Edition], London, Hodder & Stoughton

Tracy, E. (2006) *The Student's Guide to Exam Success* [2nd Edition], Oxford, Oxford University Press

Walsh, M., Chaloner, R. and Stephens, P. (2005) *Health and Social Care: AS for EDEXCEL: Student's Book*, London, Collins Educational

Walsh, M., Shackels, E., Thompson, A., Thompson, D., Chaloner, R. and Stephens, P. (2005) *Health and Social Care: A2 for EDEXCEL: Student's Book* London, Collins Educational

Walsh, M., Shackels, E., Thompson, A., Thompson, D., Chaloner, R. and Stephens, P. (2005) *Health and Social Care: A2 for EDEXCEL: Resource Pack*, London, Collins Educational

Weil, A. (2005) *Healthy Aging: A Lifelong Guide to Your Physical and Spiritual Well-Being*, New York, Alfred A. Knopf Publishers

Yorke, L. and Losquadro Liddle, T. (2003) *Why Motor Skills Matter: Improving Your Child's Physical Development to Enhance Learning and Self-Esteem*, New York, McGraw-Hill Publishing Co

Useful Websites

Action on Smoking and Health: http://www.ash.org.uk/

British Heart Foundation: http://www.bhf.org.uk

Cancer Research UK: http://www.cancerresearchuk.org/

Department of Health: http://www.dh.gov.uk

Edexcel Health & Social Care GCE A-Level: http://www.edexcel.org.uk/quals /gce/hsc /adv/9741/

FRANK Drugs Information: http://www.talktofrank.com

Human Anatomy Online: http://www.innerbody.com/index.html

National Statistics: http://www.statistics.gov.uk/

NHS: http://www.nhs.uk/

Patient UK: http://www.patient.co.uk/

Social Issues Research Centre: http://www.sirc.org/

World Health Organisation: http://www.who.int/

INDEX

Lightning Source UK Ltd.
Milton Keynes UK
UKOW021016240613

212727UK00004B/188/A